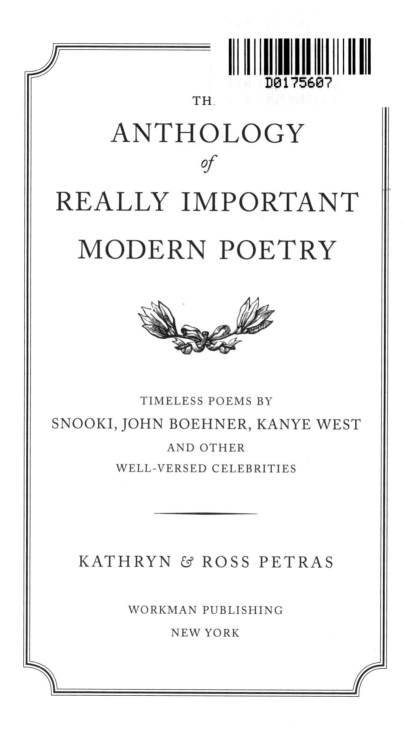

THE

ANTHOLOGY

of

REALLY IMPORTANT

MODERN POETRY

TIMELESS POEMS BY
SNOOKI, JOHN BOEHNER, KANYE WEST
AND OTHER
WELL-VERSED CELEBRITIES

KATHRYN & ROSS PETRAS

WORKMAN PUBLISHING
NEW YORK

Library of Congress Cataloging-in-Publication Data is available.

ISBN 978-0-7611-6782-2

DESIGN BY JEAN-MARC TROADEC
COVER ILLUSTRATION BY KEVIN SPROULS
ILLUSTRATIONS BY KEVIN SPROULS

The text of the "poems" in this book comprises quotations from
actual interviews, blogs, and other published sources. The authors
have formatted the quotations to make them resemble modern
verse but have not changed the words.

*Workman books are available at special discounts
when purchased in bulk for premiums and sales promotions as well as
for fund-raising or educational use. Special editions or book excerpts
also can be created to specification. For details, contact the
Special Sales Director at the address below, or send an e-mail
to specialmarkets@workman.com.*

WORKMAN PUBLISHING COMPANY, INC.
225 VARICK STREET
NEW YORK, NY 10014-4381
WWW.WORKMAN.COM

Printed in the United States of America
First printing February 2012

10 9 8 7 6 5 4 3 2 1

TABLE OF CONTENTS

ACKNOWLEDGMENTS

*W*e'd like to give special thanks to all of the Really Important People who made this book a reality: our families—Beki Petras, Sylvia Lovegren Petras and Alex Petras, and Mitch Callanan; our ever-enthusiastic agent, Andrea Somberg; and Workman's writers' Dream Team: Bruce Tracy—as always, "the bestest" of editors—Suzie Bolotin, Bob Miller, Jean-Marc Troadec, Raquel Jaramillo, Justin Krasner, Carol White, and, of course, Peter Workman, for proving that an independent publisher can be such a vital and creative force.

INTRODUCTION

*T*he time has come to celebrate the accidental lyricism of some rather unexpected wordsmiths: We speak, of course, of such heretofore grievously overlooked individuals as poet–reality star Snooki, poet-pundit Glenn Beck, poet–politician Newt Gingrich, poet–vice-president foot-in-mouth-prone Joe Biden, and many other estimable modern luminaries.

These are poet-celebrities of today, the literary voices that we can't block out because they *must* be heard.*

---

*Because they do not stop talking.

In this anthology, we've collected their (almost) timeless words—sometimes classically elegant, other times refreshingly rough-hewn, but always gripping, soulful, and eminently unforgettable.*

To help introduce you, the reader, to these fresh new voices, we've arranged the anthology by poetic schools. You will be introduced to the poems of the strangely evocative Derrièristes and those of the declining but still impactful Dictator School, among many others. We discuss the more salient tenets of each school, allowing the reader a chance to truly understand the underpinnings of the poems and, perhaps more important, the ethos from which they spring. It is this shared aesthetic and philosophical outlook that draws together and indeed weds such seemingly disparate individuals as actor Tom Cruise, mobster Big Joey Massino, and pop star Miley Cyrus (all members of the Didactic School).

*Almost.

We also discern a fascinating kinship between these modern "versifers" and their poetic ancestors. We see in Ann Coulter of the Compassionate School a faint whiff of her great predecessor, the shy and gentle recluse Emily Dickinson. We see in Rush Limbaugh, the writer of "Rushbo's Howl," another Allen Ginsberg. And, of course, in Rahm Emanuel we see another (Mametesque) Shakespeare.

The astute reader may note that some poets are acolytes of more than one school. Many critics have pondered the reason for this. Upon close analysis, we, the editors, feel this occurs because such large talent cannot be confined within the narrow strictures of one basic philosophy. So we happily find the poet Donald Trump represented not only (unsurprisingly) in the Inflated Ego School, but also (perhaps surprisingly, perhaps not) in the Religious School.

By selecting the verses to be included in this collection, we feel we have elevated them to their rightful stature. Yes, these poems are truly the important pinnacle of today's modern poetics.* This, of course, says much about the admirable state of our modern high culture.

The poems herein anthologized can now take their justified place alongside the great works of the past; they can rub shoulders, so to speak, with the sonnets of Shakespeare and, of course, the timeless epic verse of the immortal† Homer.

In closing, we invite you, the reader, to "dip in" and sip the wisdom from the troughs of these brains.

---

*Op. cit.

†Ed. note: "immortal" is here used figuratively; actually Homer died around 850 B.C.

Note: In deference to the sensibilities of our more fastidious readers, we have redacted the more Rabelaisian word choices of several of our poets. This will be signified by [REDACTED]. The astute (or worldly) reader can easily fill in the blanks.

DIDDY

THE ACTIVIST SCHOOL

*T*his poetic school is the happy result of a dovetailing between activism—work to bring about social, environmental, or political change—and creative verse. "How can I," the Poet Activist asks, "use my art and talents to make the world a better place?"

Let us turn, then, to a selection from the best of the Activist School poets.

The skeptical reader may ask: "Are they *really* making the world a better place?" We reply: "Don't ask."

DIDDY
b. 1969

The great humanitarians recognize the interconnectivity
of all life. Rapper Diddy (aka Sean "Puffy" "P. Diddy"
"Diddy" "Puff Daddy" Combs), in the spirit of the Nobel
Prize–winning Bengali poet Rabindranath Tagore,
seeks such connection through his rapping work and here,
in his poetry. It is no wonder he is so beloved.

The Importance of P

I felt like the "P" was coming between me and my fans.

We had to simplify it.

It was, you know, during concerts

    and half the crowd saying "P. Diddy"
        and half the crowd chanting "Diddy."
            Now everybody can just chant

    "Diddy."

JOHN MADDEN
b. 1936

In this spare, cryptic poem, football commentator and former coach John Madden tackles the problem of football player hydration—sagely acknowledging that man does not assuage thirst by water alone.

Liquefaction

There definitely needs to be water on the sidelines
 for these players,
but I also had some Gatorade
just in case
they were allergic to the water.

Or vice versa.

HENRY PAULSON
b. 1946

Why did then-Treasury Secretary and millionaire banker
Henry Paulson bail out his fellow bankers who were responsible
for the financial meltdown of 2008—and even let them keep their
bonuses? Paulson tackles this complex topic in a spare,
even blunt, poem that takes the intricacies of modern finance
and puts it into words we can all understand.

On Why the Little People Should Appreciate Billion Dollar Banker Bailouts

This is not just about Wall Street.
This is all about creating jobs
    growing around our country
    driving productivity
    putting capital behind ideas
        Behind people
        Behind new businesses
            small businesses . . .
There may be one or two people (but I can't think of any)
    That didn't agree with the thesis.

ALICIA SILVERSTONE
b. 1976

Actress Alicia Silverstone is to be applauded for tackling
a difficult, even controversial, topic and writing about it
with unflinching frankness. By the end of the poem, the reader
wishes that he or she, too, could take Silverstone's
helpful hand and learn to poo.

To Poo or Not to Poo

Most people aren't pooing.

> I know two girls in my life
> who are good friends,
> who were not pooing,
> but now they're pooing
> 'cause I helped them.

I taught them how to poo.

BAI LING
b. 1966

The following—a simple yet powerful poem about
a simple yet powerful contribution—is marked by its
spare language and charming acceptance
of the yoke of duty.

The Dutiful Nip Slip

If photos of my nipples
     give a little smile to others,
that is my duty.

BAI LING

Ling expands on her duty in the next poem—
taking the conscientious nipples one step further,
to the delight of the reader.

On the Inspiration for My Upcoming Book, Nipples

It's a point of view of how I see the world. Like,

> I'm wearing purple and pink, you're wearing blue;
> maybe I'm wearing red, you're wearing yellow.

> Our eyes are limited.

The book is about my perspective

> —very erotic, very intimate.

I share a lot of relationships that I had with different
gentlemen . . .

> (I wrote it in 40 days without even thinking.)

HEIDI MONTAG
b. 1986

Former reality TV star Heidi Montag offers
two tweeted tercets. Each could easily stand on its own
as a tight construct of wisdom, but when combined
they become more than the sum of their parts—a true
powerhouse of plastic surgery punditry.

Two Public Service Announcements via Twitter
(after having ten plastic surgery procedures in one day and later regretting some of them)
(particularly the excessively large implants)

1.

Giving my self a soft tissue breast massage,
Ladies
we have to keep those implants soft.

2.

Warning: to anyone who is thinking about getting their
   ears pinned
I learned after the fact it is
the most painful surgery a person can get.

THE SUSAN B. ANTHONY POETICS SCHOOL

*T*his important poetics school, named after noted feminist Susan B. Anthony, celebrates the role of modern women in today's society and seeks to put them in their proper place. At once illuminating and inspiring, the Susan B. Anthony poets are noted particularly for their nuanced sensitivity and a (somewhat) deep regard for equal rights.

TOM DELAY

b. 1947

Former Speaker of the House Tom DeLay, affectionately
nicknamed "The Hammer," wields that hammer
in this poem to hammer home a key feminist point:
Women can provide stability.*

It Takes a Woman. And More.

A woman
can take care of the family.
It takes a man

> to provide structure
> to provide stability.
> Not that a woman can't provide stability,
>   I'm not saying that . . .
>
> It does take a father, though.

*Not by themselves, though.

REAL HOUSEWIFE OF ORANGE COUNTY
ALEXIS BELLINO
b. 1976

Alexis Bellino is a "star" on reality TV show
The Real Housewives of Orange County. As such, she offers
the reader a "real" insight as to the strides made
in the women's movement, particularly in regard to
women's role in modern marriage.

My Marriage

I think America is going through
    a liberal movement,
and the older, more traditional marriage values
    are becoming something of the past.
Jim and I are one couple who still favor
    a more traditional marriage
rather than a liberal marriage, and because we do,
    it makes my marriage an interesting conversation
        topic.

However just because we have a more traditional marriage
does not mean I do not make my own decisions.

As you can see just in this one episode,
    I chose to wear the dress I wanted,
not the dress
    that was Jim's first choice.

KING ABDULLAH OF SAUDI ARABIA

b. 1923

A simple yet resonant poem by the ruler
of Saudi Arabia, "The Rights of Women" offers
an enlightened international view.

The Rights of Women

I believe strongly in the rights of women.
 My mother is a woman,
 my sister is a woman,
 my daughter is a woman,
 my wife is a woman.

I believe the day will come when women drive.
 (The issue will require patience.
 In time, I believe it will be possible.
 And
 I believe
 patience is a virtue.)

RUSH LIMBAUGH
b. 1951

The final example of leading poets in the
Susan B. Anthony School is the following work by pundit
Rush Limbaugh. Consider this a manifesto, if you will,
of the enlightened conservative male regarding the woman
of today, and savor the verbal wink at the end.

I Just Flew In From Vegas and, Boy, Are My Arms Tired

I'm a huge supporter of women. What I'm not is a
    supporter of liberalism.
        Feminism is what I oppose.
                Feminism has led women astray.
I love the women's movement
    especially when walking behind it.

THE COMPASSIONATE POETS

*T*he Compassionate Poets dig deep into the wellspring of empathy, exploring the pain that exists in the world. By so doing, they in effect "defang the serpent" and lead us to truly appreciate the generous nature of the human spirit.

Ed. note: The school numbers among its practitioners many top banking executives, politicians, and the like. This is not surprising, since, as we are frequently advised on television, these politicians, bankers, and corporate executives so deeply care for all of us.

JOHN BOEHNER

b. 1949

Some may accuse the Speaker of the House
of sentimentalism, but we detect genuine compassion
and concern for all the little people.*

Feelings, Nothing More Than Feelings

I've got real empathy for those who
      are unemployed,
as most of you know
      I've got 11 brothers and sisters.
I know that three of my brothers lost their jobs,
      I'm not sure whether they've found jobs yet,
so
I've got a lot of empathy for those caught in this
  economic downturn.

*Including his own brothers and sisters.†

  †Those whom he can recall.

HARRY REID
b. 1939

After reading this short poem by Sen. Harry Reid,
the reader is tempted to yell Hoorah!

Harry Reid and the Very Big Day

Today is a big day
in America.
Only 36,000 people
lost their jobs today.

CARL–HENRIC SVANBERG
b. 1952

A starkly simple message in a starkly worded poem.
The reader feels the figurative embrace of the poet, who also serves
proudly as the chairman of oil pollution giant British Petroleum
(BP), and, of course, feels his heartfelt sincerity.

BP Stands for Beautiful People

I hear comments sometimes
that large oil companies are greedy companies
or don't care.
But that is not the case with BP:

We CARE about the small people.

NATALIE PORTMAN
b. 1981

Who better to explore the positive and, indeed, thrilling
side of a recession than a millionaire actress?

Exciting Times for the Unhappily Employed, the Underemployed, and the Unemployed

I think it's kind of an exciting time. I mean,
everyone is cutting back.
It's happening in every industry—including our own.
All of a sudden,

> people are doing jobs that they hate and
> they're not making as much money
> as they thought they would or
> they've lost their jobs entirely.

JAMES CAMERON
b. 1954

Juxtaposition is king of the poem, if you will,
in film director James Cameron's short tribute to
those who lost their lives on the *Titanic*.

After Winning an Oscar for the Film Titanic

This is for a real event that happened when real
    people died
and shocked the world in 1912 and I'd like . . .
to do a few seconds of silence
in remembrance of 1,500 men, women and children
    who died.
You really made this a night to remember in every way.
Now let's party 'til dawn!

ALAN DERSHOWITZ
b. 1938

Lawyer Alan Dershowitz opens his poetic piehole
in this lyrical work on a sensitive topic.

Sing, O Muse,
of the American Way of Torture

I would talk about nonlethal torture, say
    a sterilized needle underneath the nail,
    which would violate the Geneva Accords,
    but you know

countries all over the world violate the Geneva Accords.

> *They do it secretly and hypothetically, the way the*
> *French did it in Algeria. If we ever came close to*
> *doing it . . .*

> I think we would want to do it
> with accountability and openly . . .

> Candor and accountability in a democracy is
>   very important.

ANN COULTER
b. 1961

In what is at once a poem of compassion
and one of visionary force, Ann Coulter puckishly
reminds us that girls just want to have fun—
even in the face of international strife.

My Kind of Fun

I'm getting a little fed up with hearing about,
oh,
civilian casualties.
I think we ought to nuke North Korea right now
just to give the rest of the world a warning . . .
I just think it would be fun to
nuke them.

THE CONSTITUTIONAL POETS

*T*he Constitutional Poets strive to elucidate the true (and sometimes deeply hidden) meaning of the American Constitution and the rights therein. Most often these Constitutional truths as seen through their highly creative minds bear little or no resemblance to that which we were taught in school and in universities. This is probably due to the deplorable state of legal education at major universities such as Harvard and Stanford, which have not graduated even one Constitutional Poet.

MICHAEL SAVAGE
b. 1942

Radio talk show host Michael Savage here
marries the politically poetic with the eminently practical.
What is the role of government in private matters?
Note Savage's deft use of the word *fuck* while addressing
this topic, and his clever shift from verb to adverb.

The Role of the Government by a Lover of the Constitution of the United States of America

I'm not teaching my children how to
    fuck.
There's no need for that.
And I don't want the government teaching my kids how to
    fuck.
Do I want a bunch of wack jobs at school with
    cucumbers
    and dolls teaching it to our kids?
No fucking way!

RAND PAUL
b. 1963

What are the basic rights of a citizen of the United States? Here, in this heartfelt poem, Sen. Rand Paul astutely homes in on the real question: What basic rights should be denied to a citizen of the United States?

*Free Me, O Lord,
from Government Health Care*

With regard to the idea of whether you have
    a right to health care,
you have to realize what that implies.
    It's not an abstraction.
    I'm a physician.

        That means you have a right to come to my
          house and conscript me.
IT MEANS YOU BELIEVE IN SLAVERY.
It means that you're going to enslave not only
me, but
    the janitor at my hospital,
      the person who cleans my office,
        the assistants who work in my
          office,
          the nurses. . . .
          You have a right to beat
          down my door with the
police,
escort me away and force me to take care of you?
That's ultimately what the right to free health care
    would be.

GLEN URQUHART*
b. 1948

Glen Urquhart (the Tea Party–backed Republican nominee
for the Delaware House seat) takes the literary trope
of opening a poem with a question. It is a question that has
engaged legal scholars for years, but Urquhart
has the—possibly surprising—answer.

A Poetic Discourse on the Separation of Church and State

Do you know, where does this phrase "separation of
   Church and State" come from?

It was not in Jefferson's letter to the Danbury Baptists. . . .

> The exact phrase "separation of Church and State"
>   came out of
> Adolf Hitler's mouth,
> *That's* where it comes from.

So the next time your liberal friends talk about
the separation of Church and State—

—ask them why they're

Nazis.

*Note: Interestingly, Glen Urquhart is also a glen in the Highland
Council area of Scotland.

TED NUGENT
b. 1948

Ted Nugent, a rocker and crossbow-hunting aficionado, takes
aim for the jugular in this pithy, exhortative poem.
It is said that his audience at his first reading of this—at an NRA
convention—rose to their feet cheering. One can imagine why.

American Constitutional Values

Remember the Alamo!
Shoot 'em!
I want the bad guys dead.

No court case.
No parole.
No early release.

I want 'em dead.
Get a gun and when they attack you,
shoot 'em.

GIUSEPPE "JOEY" GAMBINA
b. 1969

In this radiant tercet, mobster Joey Gambina
takes on the ramifications of an intrusive
unconstitutional government.

Why I Don't Kiss My Consigliere No More

We don't kiss in public
    no more.

The government's taking pictures.

THE DERRIÈRISTES

*S*ome poets see inspiration in a sunrise, in the dew quivering on a leaf after a gentle spring rain; others find it in more prosaic (yet still natural) things.

Enter the Derrièristes. These earthy poets "look below"—focusing specifically on the buttocks for poetic inspiration.

GWYNETH PALTROW
b. 1972

With a temporal theme of change by way of
buttock observation, Gwyneth Paltrow's "The Bottom Line"
celebrates both acceptance and mutability.

The Bottom Line

My butt!
My butt,
      butt,
            butt.

Tracy met me, she said that I had

a long, square butt

that she was going to redesign,
and I was, like, "Yeah? Good luck."

The amazing thing is she was right!

And it's still changing!

WILL SMITH
b. 1968

Actor Will Smith approaches his Derrièriste verse
with a distinctively sassy style—as distinctively sassy
as the "special butt" he writes about.

Mine Is Special

I have a special butt. It has special
     curves and it kinda has
     its own attitude . . .
I think the audience can feel that,
and if I were to put someone else's butt in that place,
the audience would feel cheated and emotionally insulted.

KIM KARDASHIAN
b. 1980

Kim Kardashian, primarily celebrated for her
shapely buttocks, here pays them a personal tribute.
As with her TV show, this is pure art.

Butt Acceptance

I see ridiculous stories about my butt,
like how it has been insured.
I feel like saying, "Hey, everyone has a butt.
It's not that big a deal!"
    But I suppose it's flattering.

Personally, I've always loved the curvy look.
Even when I was a little girl and all my friends would be
like, "Oh, my god,
your butt's so big."
And I'd say,
    "I love it."

GISELE BÜNDCHEN
b. 1980

Model Gisele Bündchen reveals—or chooses not to reveal—her *bunda* (as she might call it in her native Brazilian Portuguese) in this highly personal poem.

Special Occasions

I make sure that they understand that
My booty has to be covered.
It's my booty
and I feel like when you're walking on the runway,
    God knows where they're looking.
It's not that I feel self-conscious,
It's that I feel like
    my booty
    should be shown on
    special occasions.
    For special people.

THE "DES FESSES, JE NE PARLE PAS" SCHOOL

*O*ne may argue that no, buttocks are not everything. Thus, the "Des Fesses, Je Ne Parle Pas" (in English, "Of the Buttocks, I Do Not Speak") School. These poets celebrate other important areas in the American body politic—most notably the vagina and the breast.

Breast poems, unlike the more typical vagina poems, usually focus on a single concept: Size. (Of breasts.) Despite this single focus, the poems are marked by breathtaking creative variety. Clearly, one size does *not* fit all!

ROBERT PATTINSON
b. 1986

Actor Robert Pattinson reflects on his
unique and metaphorical allergy, possibly a first
in modern American poetry.

Photo Shoots, Nude Women & Me

I really hate vaginas.

I'm allergic to vagina.

But I can't say I had no idea, because it was a 12-hour shoot,

so you kind of get the picture that these women are going to stay naked after, like, five or six hours.

But I wasn't exactly prepared.

I had no idea what to say to these girls.

Thank God I was hung over.

DREW BARRYMORE
b. 1975

Actress Drew Barrymore comes to an intriguing
conclusion regarding large breasts.

Upon Pondering Breasts

When they're huge,
    you become very self-conscious . . .
I've learned something, though,
    through my years of pondering and pontificating,
      and that is:
Men love them, and I love that.

CARMEN ELECTRA
b. 1972

For those who are not blessed
with Drew Barrymore–size mammaries, model/
entertainer Carmen Electra reflects on artificial
augmentation in this poem of nostalgia
and memories of the way they were.

From 32B to 36D

I had nice boobs before—
they were small but
nice . . . Of course
I could have them reduced.
But
      then where would I be?

CHERYL COLE
b. 1983

Is larger better? This important question
is explored in this stark modern poem
by pop singer Cheryl Cole.

In an Ideal World

In an ideal world I'd have smaller boobs.
I'm a 32D
which is ridiculous for my size
and boobs are hard to dress.
I hate looking booby.
You can look
really cheap
very
quickly.

KATE MOSS
b. 1974

Model Kate Moss has grown breasts.
She ponders their meaning in this lightly
philosophical poetic reflection.

Spring Awakening

I've just started wearing bras.
It's a miracle.
Great timing for my lingerie collection.
I've just grown breasts.

I am a woman now.
It's true.
Honestly, I've never worn a bra in my life.
Ever!

It's so awful, even my friends are phoning me up and
  saying, "Are you pregnant?"
And I'm like, "No! I just put on a couple of pounds and
  they went in the right place."
Isn't that weird?
Now I can fill a B cup.

My boyfriend might not like them.

I'm a bit worried.

JUSTIN BIEBER
b. 1994

Youthful performer Justin Bieber tips his hat to
the Belle of Amherst in this poem—expressing a somewhat
conventional idea in a very unconventional, even
idiosyncratic, way. The reader will not think of how a girl
smells the same way again.

The Biebs Hearts Emily Dickinson

Let's be Real—the way
a girl smells
is Very Important—
to a Guy!

CASTRO

THE DICTATOR SCHOOL

*T*he Dictator School is a most exclusive school of poetry. To be included among its members, the poet must be (or have been) a working dictator. As there are only several hundred nations in the world and so many are democracies, the Dictator Poet is a rarity. Yet those few more than make up for their sparse number by their immense output—they are among the most prolific (some may also say verbose) of poets. One possible reason for this: As dictators, they can shoot editors and critics, while other writers and poets can only wish to.

SADDAM HUSSEIN

1937–2006

Ever the innovator, creative provocateur Saddam Hussein
of Iraq broke new ground in that classic poetic motif:
human-bear sexual relations.

Unbearable Desire

Even an animal respects a man's desire, if it wants to
   copulate with him.
Doesn't a female bear try to please a herdsman
      when she drags him into the mountains as it
         happens in the North of Iraq?
      She drags him into her den, so that he, obeying her
         desire, would copulate with her.
Doesn't she bring him nuts, gathering them from the trees
   or picking them from the bushes?
      Doesn't she climb into the houses of farmers in order
         to steal some cheese, nuts, and even raisins,
      so that she can feed the man
      and awake in him the desire to have her?

KIM JONG IL

1941–2011

North Korean dictator Kim Jong Il was more than simply a Dictator Poet. He was also, as the following poem demonstrates, an insightful critic of other art forms. Of particular note: his inspired use of his "day job" (i.e., dictating, or being Supreme Leader) as a parallel for that of film director. The reader will not only grasp the thrust of the apparently fascinating *Juche**-inspired system of directing but will also gain a deeper understanding of the system by which one remains the Dear Leader (to use another of Kim Jong Il's preferred *noms-de-travail*) of a large peninsular country.

Let Me Bore You At Length About My Theories of Film Directing

In film directing,
the basic factor is also to work well with the
    artists,
    technicians
    and production
    and supply personnel
who are directly involved in film-making.

This is the essential requirement of the *Juche*-inspired
    system of directing.

---

*Kim's father's philosophy of North Korean self-reliance (based mostly on getting a lot of Soviet and Chinese aid).

This system is our system of directing
> under which the director becomes the commander of
>> the creative group and pushes ahead with creative
>> work as a whole in a coordinated way,
> giving precedence to political work and putting the
>> main emphasis on working with the people who
>> make films.

This system embodies the fundamental features of the
socialist system
> and the basic principle of the *Juche* idea that man is
>> the master of everything and decides everything.

Hence, it fully conforms with the collective nature of film-
making
> and the characteristic features of direction.

MUAMMAR EL-QADDAFI

1942–2011

Here, deposed dictator and lay scientist
Muammar el-Qaddafi of Libya explains menstruation,
sagely noting that males do not menstruate.

The Sexes: A Poetical Scientific Examination of Crucial Differences

Women are females
and
men are males.
According to gynaecologists, women menstruate
every month or so,
while men,
being male,
do not menstruate or suffer during the monthly period.
A woman,
being a female,
is naturally subject to monthly bleeding.
When a woman does not menstruate,
she is pregnant.
If she is pregnant, she becomes,
due to pregnancy,
less active
for about a year.

HUGO CHAVEZ
b. 1954

Hugo Chavez as elected president of Venezuela
served as only a quasi-dictator but, according to many accounts,
vied for full status. His poem below, though brief, demonstrates
why his promotion to full Dictator Poet would indeed
be "out of this world."

Deep Thoughts on Deep Space

I have always said—heard—that it would not be strange
that there had been civilization on Mars,
but maybe
capitalism arrived there,
imperialism arrived
and finished off the planet.

FIDEL CASTRO
b. 1926

This poem is one of Cuban dictator Fidel Castro's greatest. It was recited—over the course of about an hour—at an official function commemorating the 52nd anniversary of an assault on enemy garrisons. *(Ed. note: Due to space constrictions, we have been forced to truncate the poem—which contained hundreds of stanzas, including unexpected digressions on coffee mill production and a particularly gripping section on nonferrous metallurgy.)*

Many, Many Things

I thank our generous and heroic people
for the privilege of commemorating this
    anniversary . . .
The Revolution today is experiencing a moment
  worthy of that
    memorable date.

More than
3 million 100 thousand pressure cookers,
3 million 500 thousand rice steamers,
3 million 100 thousand electric pressure cookers,
3 million 800 thousand electric hobs and
1 million 100 thousand 12-inch fans
have been purchased.

More than
5 million 300 thousand gaskets for refrigerators,
650 thermostats and
7 million gaskets for coffee makers
have also been bought . . .

Condemn us, it doesn't matter, history will absolve us.

RAÚL CASTRO
b. 1931

Castro's brother Raúl took over the mantle of dictator, and also that of poet, from his brother. Sadly, many feel that he is not the versatile versifier Fidel is. One may note how he mimics his brother (listing the number of grocery stores, the percentages, numbers of municipalities, even liters of milk sold), yet the Fidelian magic somehow eludes him.

Many Many Things Otra Vez

Last June 30th, the consumers registered in
    5,361 grocery stores,
that is, 49 percent of those in the 154 municipalities
that could implement this procedure
were receiving milk this way.
Actually, 52 million liters of milk were sold in this way
in the first six months of this year.

Additionally, 1,800 tons of fuel has been saved
whose value exceeds 2,350,000 dollars.
This fuel saving could increase every year
with the expansion of this direct milk distribution
    procedure.

Efforts are also being made to improve the organization
    of cargo transportation
since it is a fact that an adequate operation allows for
    a 20 percent fuel saving.

Besides, an experience is under way
in sixteen municipalities
which consists in centralizing the transportation used for
   this purpose
at that level,
except in those cases where it is not logical
due to the type of vehicles used or
the nature of the work they do.
The results are showing that the work can be done
with 30 percent of the cargo transportation operated today.

We shall continue to advance with this experience
at a pace that can guarantee its rigorous application
to avoid spoiling the idea,
which, by the way,
has had to face some people's useless resistance.

CRUISE

THE DIDACTIC SCHOOL: INSIGHTS ON A VARIETY OF SUBJECTS BY THE POET AS TEACHER

*T*he Didactic Poet is Poet as Teacher. His or her work offers instruction on a wide range of subjects, from the practical to the philosophical, from the micro to the macro, from the prosaic to the sublime. The following works will at once entertain, elucidate, evoke, educate . . . and, more important, enlighten. And edify, too.

TOM CRUISE
b. 1962

Who better to explain the vagaries of the complex medical
science of psychiatry in verse than the triple threat of movie star-
historian-scientist that is Tom Cruise? Note Cruise's sly homage
to Dante's *Inferno* in this poem by addressing his words to "Matt"—
who is, in effect, Virgil to Tom's Dante . . . or is it vice versa?
Has Cruise cleverly turned a tried-and-true medieval literary trope
(that of inclusion of a literary überguide) on its ear?

An Exegesis on Psychiatry by an Historian of the Science

I've never agreed with psychiatry, ever.
Before I was a Scientologist I never agreed with psychiatry.
And when I started studying the *history* of psychiatry,
    I understood more and more
why I didn't believe in psychology.

And as far as the Brooke Shields thing is, look.
You gotta understand,
I really care about Brooke Shields.
I—I think here's a—a—a wonderful and talented woman.
And—I wanna see her do well.
And I know that— psychiatry is—is a pseudoscience.
Matt, you have to understand this.
Here we are today where I talk out against drugs and
    psychiatric abuses of electric-shocking people, okay,
    against their will,
of drugging children with them not knowing the effects
    of these drugs.

Do you know what Adderall is? Do you know Ritalin?
    Do you know now that Ritalin is a street drug?
    Do you understand that?
No.
You see.
Here's the problem:
You don't know the history of psychiatry.
I do.

All it does is mask the problem, Matt.
And if you understand the history of it,
    it masks the problem.
That's what it does.
That's all it does.
You're not getting to the reason why.
There is no such thing as a chemical imbalance ...
The thing that I'm saying about Brooke is that
    there's misinformation, okay.
And she doesn't understand the history of psychiatry.
She ... she doesn't understand in the same way that
        you don't understand it,
        Matt.

ALEX RODRIGUEZ
b. 1975

Similarly, baseball star Alex Rodriguez turns his
able pen to matters mental. A-Rod, however, prefers the
simpler "jock" approach, utilizing a haiku-like style
in contrast to Cruise's more complex and intricate verse.

A Good Thing

Therapy can be
    a good thing,
It can be
      therapeutic.

PRINCE PHILIP
b. 1921

This, a sociological offering from an international traveler, is written in the form of an old Anglo-Saxon oral tradition—the "riddle" poem.

The Royal Gastronome

If it has got four legs
    and it is not a chair,
if it has got two wings and it flies
    but is not an aeroplane,
and if it swims
    and is not a submarine,
the Cantonese will eat it.

KANYE WEST
b. 1977

Rapper Kanye West offers this for all those
readers (and one can only assume there are many)
who have wondered about combs. (Note: West is
addressing the grooming tool, not his fellow rapper Sean
"Puffy" "P. Diddy" "Diddy" "Puff Daddy" Combs.)

A Lyrical Examination of Combs

Combs have been on the scene ever since humans had hair
    on his head.
which is quite some time?
The date
    perhaps
goes beyond the time of the Old Stone Age.

Man being man
    and not a lion
would not be content to let his mane run wild and free.
        So he had to find some ways to tame it.

First on the list of combing operations must have been
    the use of fingers. So in a way
        the fingers
    are
    the first combs
    of history.

Today, combs are universal and no corner of the globe
    is without it.

BRISTOL PALIN
b. 1990

In her "Thoughts," Bristol Palin ably—and lyrically—
demonstrates why she became an abstinence foundation's
spokesperson and an ambassador to American youth.
One is urged to pay special attention to her use of "like"
and "uh" as a means not only of underscoring her points
but also of identifying with her youthful audience.

Thoughts on Abstinence from a $265,000 a Year Abstinence Advocate

I think abstinence is like, like the,
    uh,
I don't know how to put it, like, the main,
everyone should be abstinent
or whatever
    but it's not realistic at all.
Regardless of what I did personally,
I just think that abstinence is the only way that you
   can effectively,
    uh,
foolproof way to prevent pregnancy . . .
    I just wanna go out there and promote abstinence.

IVANA TRUMP
b. 1949

Here, Mrs. Donald Trump, or rather a former Mrs. Trump, lyrically
explains her child-raising philosophy in this didactic masterpiece.
Notice how the poet utilizes a powerful parallel construction to illumine
the theme of childhood sports; i.e., some sports are "good," some
are "bad," in terms of future earning power.*

My Recipe for Raising Kids

My recipe for raising kids:
I encourage my children to try new things.

As much as I tell them they can do anything,
I don't want them to engage in pastimes that have no future.

> The other day, Ivanka came to me and said
> she wanted to enroll one afternoon in field hockey.
> I said,
> "Ivanka, that's a boy's sport. There's no future in
> it for you."

If Ivanka wanted to do karate, fine.
Field hockey she doesn't need.
Golf, I think, is a perfect sport, but fencing? I'd say,
> "Kid, don't waste your time."

Ice skating is great exercise and it's social.
> You won't get many phone calls to play field hockey,
> but ice skating you can do in New York
> at the beautiful Wollman Rink in Central Park
> which their father and I rebuilt during our marriage.

*Ed. note: The child in question, Ivanka, is now a multimillionaire.

JOSEPH "BIG JOEY" MASSINO
b. 1943

Mobster Big Joey uses a deceptively simple
trope—the repetition of a phrase—to lead the reader
into a "hands-on" learning experience.

The Meat in the Gravy

You never talk in a club,
you never talk in a car,
you never talk on a cell phone,
you never talk on a phone,
you never talk in your house.

You can't be a father and a son in the same crew.
It don't work . . .
You can't be afraid to be [in] the top seat.
I wasn't afraid . . .

If you need somebody to kill somebody,
you need workers
     —it takes all kinds of meat to make a good sauce.

COOLIO
b. 1963

"Bullshit!" rapper Coolio yells in answer to his
own question. The reader will agree.

Technological Musings Involving Microbiotics

All this technology. You think it came from this planet? . . .
Bullshit!
I don't think
men are that smart.
I think
it came from somewhere else . . .
Microbiotics,
     computer science,
         jet planes—
              they came from a different planet.

GORDON RAMSAY
b. 1966

With a twinkle in his eye and a puckish choice
of words, chef Ramsay teaches us more than we ever
knew about scallops and nonstick surfaces.

Teflon Nightmare

Missy!

If you sauté scallops
in a nonstick pan,
they won't stick.

That's why it's called
fucking nonstick!

I don't know what they call it in Texas,
sweetheart,
but fuck me!

VINCENT "VINNY GORGEOUS" BASCIANO
b. 1959

Mafia boss Vinny Gorgeous takes an unadorned straightforward
approach in his "Being a Hoodlum." Its simplicity, however,
is somewhat misleading, as his subject matter (comparing hoodlums
to businessmen) and conclusion are rather sophisticated.

Being a Hoodlum

If you're a hoodlum,
Louie,
    I can show you the right direction.
We can make money.

But if you're a businessman,
I can't show you how
to be a hoodlum.

You can teach a hoodlum how
    to be a businessman,
but you can't take a businessman and teach him how
    to be a hoodlum.

    It's a lot easier to train a hoodlum.

ANTHONY WEINER
b. 1964

There are those who feel former U.S. Representative Anthony Weiner does not belong among the Didactic School's members, chiefly because his work is addressed to a specific individual (a porn star) about a specific occasion (that of receiving sexually creative messages from him). We, however, feel that in spite of the specificity, the lesson is universal—at least for all congresspeople.

To a Lasciviously Sexted Porn Star: A Short Discourse on What to Say to the Press

The key is to have a short, thought-out statement
that tackles the top-line questions and then refer people
    back to it.
Have a couple of iterations of:
        This is silly.
        Like so many others, I follow Rep. Weiner on
            Twitter.
        I don't know him and have never met him.
        He briefly followed me and sent me a dm saying
            thank you for the follow.
        That's it.

    And then maybe insert
    some y'alls
    in there.

MILEY CYRUS
b. 1992

Pop sensation Miley Cyrus proves she is also a poetic
pundit in this simple yet punchy piece.

Osculatory Musings

If you look at the picture,
    I'm turned away,
    and he's kissing me on the cheek.
It's very hilarious to me that people say
    "They're making out."
In making out, there's
    a tongue.

SARAH PALIN
b. 1964

Sarah Palin fittingly evokes the great American
poet Walt Whitman in this sprawling poetic paean to her
sprawling home state. Her celebration of the hard
"manly man" virtues found in the state would certainly
have pleased Whitman, who was noted for
the subtle homosexual undertones in his works.

If Walt Whitman Were a Woman from Wasilla, or O (Former) Governor! My (Former) Governor!

The rugged rugged hardy people that live up here and
some of the most patriotic people whom you will ever
know live here,

And one thing that you are known for is your steadfast
support of our military community up here and I thank
you for that

And thank you United States military for protecting the
greatest nation on Earth.

Together we stand.

And getting up here I say it is the best road trip in America soaring through nature's finest show. Denali, the great one, soaring under the midnight sun and then the extremes.

In the wintertime it's the frozen road that is competing with the view of ice fogged frigid beauty, the cold though, doesn't it split the Cheechakos from the Sourdoughs?

And then in the summertime such extreme summertime about a hundred and fifty degrees hotter than just some months ago, than just some months from now,

With fireweed blooming along the frost heaves and merciless rivers that are rushing and carving and reminding us that here,

Mother Nature wins.

It is as throughout all Alaska that big wild good life teeming along the road that is north to the future. That is what we get to see every day.

Now what the rest of America gets to see along with us is in this last frontier there is hope and opportunity and there is country pride.

And it is our men and women in uniform securing it, and we are facing tough challenges in America with some seeming to just be Hell bent maybe on tearing down our nation,

Perpetuating some pessimism, and suggesting American apologetics, suggesting perhaps that

Our best days were yesterdays . . .

And first, some straight talk for some, just some in the media because another right protected for all of us is freedom of the press,

and you all have such important jobs reporting facts and informing the electorate, and exerting power to influence.

You represent what could and should be a respected honest profession that could and should be the cornerstone of our democracy.

Democracy depends on you, and that is why, that's why our troops are willing to die for you. So, how 'bout in honor of the American soldier,

Ya quit makin' things up . . .

Let me tell you, Alaskans really need to stick together on this with new leadership in this area especially, encouraging new leadership.

Got to stiffen your spine to do what's right for Alaska when the pressure mounts, because you're going to see anti-hunting, anti-second-amendment circuses from Hollywood and here's how they do it.

They use these delicate, tiny, very talented celebrity starlets, they use Alaska as a fundraising tool for their anti-second-amendment causes.

Stand strong, and remind them patriots will protect our guaranteed, individual right to bear arms, and by the way, Hollywood needs to know,

We eat, therefore we hunt.

THE EXPLANATORY POETS

*L*ess a formal school than a point of view, the Explanatory Poets (also called the Poets of Explanation) use their verses to explain. But this is a deceptively simplistic explanation, if you will, for as the poets explain, they simultaneously *deny*. It is this which makes this form of poetry actually a rather complex one. "What is truth?" Pontius Pilate famously asked. These poems supply the answer.

. . . Or do they?

GEORGE ALAN REKERS
b. 1948

When questioned about his traveling companion,
antigay activist George Alan Rekers turned to verse in this
masterful haiku. (Note the perfect adherence to the
classic 5-7-5 syllabic structure, as well as the deft handling
of the "kireji"—or cutting word—*that's*.)

After Being Caught in a Miami Airport Traveling with a Male Escort from RentBoy.com

I had surgery
    and I can't lift luggage. *That's*
why I hired him.

MAHMOUD AHMADINEJAD
b. 1956

When questioned about the treatment of gays in Iran,
Iranian president Mahmoud Ahmadinejad also turned to verse
in this masterful quintain. (Some critics posit that
Ahmadinejad's choice of a five-line structure is a playful
oneupmanship of notable Persian poet Omar Khayyam's
famous four-line quatrains.)

Denial Is Not Just a River in Egypt

In Iran, we don't have homosexuals,
like in your country.

We don't have that in our country.
In Iran, we do not have this phenomenon.

I don't know who's told you that we have it.

HILLARY CLINTON
b. 1947

Hillary Clinton's poem of explanation is marked
by a particularly intricate parsing—vaguely reminiscent of the
famous "It depends on what the meaning of the word *is* is."

A Poem of Denying Charges That I Asked My Former Aide to Fire White House Office Staff, or, Denial Is Not Just a River in Arkansas

He doesn't say I directly told him
    anything.
He says that,
you know, the fact that I expressed
concern
    had an impact on him.
    The mere expression of
        concern
could be, I guess, taken to
mean something
more
    than it was meant.

HILLARY CLINTON

Here, Ms. Clinton turns her explanatory poetic
talents to new forms. In a fascinating hybrid of modern form
with a nod to the best of 18th-century narrative poesy,
she denies charges that she "faked" a harrowing experience
to sound more impressive while on the campaign trail.

The Bosnia Cantos

Part I: In which the poet recounts her frightening experiences:

I remember landing under sniper fire.
There was supposed to be some kind of a greeting
  ceremony at the airport,
    but instead
we just ran with our heads down to get into the
  vehicles to get to our base.

*Part II: In which, after being informed this isn't the way it
happened, the poet now re-recounts her experiences:*

Now let me tell you what I can remember, OK
—because what I was told was that we had to land a
  certain way and move quickly because of the threat
  of sniper fire.
So I misspoke . . .
if I said something that made it seem as though
  there was actual fire
    —that's not what I was told.
      I was told we had to land a certain way,
        (we had to have our bulletproof
          stuff on because of the threat of
          sniper fire.

I was also told that the greeting ceremony had been
    moved away from the tarmac
but that there was this eight-year-old girl
and, I can't, I can't rush by her,
I've got to at least greet her
—so I greeted her, I took her stuff
and then I left)
                Now that's my memory of it.

*Part III: In which the poet explains that it doesn't matter what
her memories were or weren't.*

I think that a minor blip,
You know,
    if I said something that,
you know,
    I say a lot of things
        —millions of words a day—
           so if I misspoke it was
just a misstatement.

ERIC MASSA
b. 1959

Rep. Eric Massa, asked about his inappropriate
groping of male staffers, takes a more prolix
approach in his explanatory verse.

Groping, Groping Towards the Truth

Okay. So, we're at a wedding, New Year's Eve.
> Everyone had too much to drink.
> There were 300 people there. I went with a
> > bridesmaid, danced with her, sat down. I went
> > > back to my staff,
> all the bachelors.

They all make the remarks that you can imagine about
> you ought to do this,
> you ought to do that.

I grabbed the guy and tousled his hair and say,
> I ought to do it to you.

And there are other words and they're all out there.
> I gave a full and complete disclosure
> > and I left because I realized the party was getting to
> > a place that I shouldn't be at.

And I did it.

Now, they're saying I groped a male staffer.
Yes, I did. Not only did I grope him,
I tickled him until he couldn't breathe and four guys
> jumped on top of me.
> > It was my 50th birthday.

SILVIO BERLUSCONI
b. 1936

Former Prime Minister of Italy Silvio Berlusconi,
needs no introduction, especially to nubile young women,
to whom he quite readily introduces himself, often
sans pants. His poem of explanation actually elucidates
precisely this—i.e., meeting nubile young women,
supposedly sans pants.

Il Vecchio Sporcaccione 1

The girls were just
shaking a leg in the disco
—alone,
as I've never liked dancing . . .
Besides . . . how can it be that someone pays for a sexual
    performance via bank transfer?

SILVIO BERLUSCONI

Similarly, Berlusconi's second Dirty Old Man poem
focuses on the young and nubile—and poignantly evokes
a Whittier*-esque "it might have been" sense of regret.

Il Vecchio Sporcaccione 2

Even though I am a little brat
33 girls in two months seems like
too much.

Even for a 30-year-old.
It's too much
For anybody.

*John Greenleaf.

OBAMA

THE HAIKU
PRACTITIONERS

---

*C*an one express a feeling or evoke a mood or paint a verbal picture in only three lines and seventeen syllables? This is the arduous task faced by the modern haiku masters, poets who have chosen to follow the ancient Japanese tradition of haiku poetry. But they bring to this, of course, a modern twist: They often opt for not only small poems but, most innovatively, also small ideas.

EMMITT SMITH
b. 1969

The following, by football player/commentator
Emmitt Smith, shows that he has mastered not only
the Japanese haiku form but also the
Japanese Zen philosophy.

Tautologically Speaking, Tautly Put

I think it's his self-
    confidence in himself that
makes him confident.

PARIS HILTON
b. 1981

Socialite Paris Hilton chooses a *senryu*—a poem
with haiku structure, but one that focuses on human
beings rather than nature—to write about her
usual topic, Paris Hilton.

My Life: A Senryu

A living—I get
    Paid to go to events and
Parties, and it's fun!

MARIAH CAREY
b. 1970

Proving that she has quite a handle on the poetic form, here singer Mariah Carey, whose work falls into several different poetic schools, pens a perfectly crafted—and timeless—haiku.

On Time

I disregard time.
You don't see me wear a watch.
    —I don't have birthdays.

BARACK OBAMA
b. 1961

The poet-president uses a reverse haiku arrangement—a 7-5-7 syllabic arrangement rather than traditional 5-7-5—in this creative masterpiece on the contentious Middle East. *(Ed. note: Both Arab and Israeli critics have commented on the skillfully uncontroversial treatment of the topic.)*

Indisputable: A Hokku-Like Thought

Let me be absolutely
   clear: Israel is
   a strong friend of Israel's.

SIMPSON

THE HYGIENISTS

*T*he Hygienist School is the modern successor to the Naturalist writing of Balzac and Flaubert—but it takes it all to the next level: transforming naturalist prose into poetry and adding an important dose of personal hygiene (or nonhygiene, as the case may be). The result: poems about life as it is really lived—and who lives without being aware of personal hygiene (or nonhygiene, as the case may be) issues?

HARRY REID
b. 1939

Sen. Harry Reid boldly goes where no senator has
(publicly) gone before in this evocative poem.
We are lucky indeed that Reid did not listen to his staff
and chose instead to share his true olfactory
feelings about his constituents.

The Scent of a Nation

My staff tells me not to say this,
>   but I'm going to say it anyway—
In the summer because of the heat and high humidity,
you could literally
>   SMELL
the tourists coming into the Capitol.

ROBERT PATTINSON
b. 1986

Actor Robert Pattinson's poem falls into the
philosophical branch of the Hygienists. While on one hand
examining his personal shampooing habits, it also looks
at the philosophical: to wit, what is hair actually for?

A Philosophy of Follicular
Fastidiousness
(Or, My Hair Is Greasy)

I don't really see the point in washing your hair.

If you don't care if your hair's clean or not, then why would
you wash it?

It's like,

I don't clean my apartment 'cause I don't care.

I have my apartment for sleeping in

and

I have my hair for just, you know, hanging out on my head.

JESSICA SIMPSON
b. 1980

Like Pattinson, singer/actress Jessica Simpson
homes in on one important aspect of herself—her toothbrushing
habits. Unlike Pattinson, though, Simpson remains the
refreshing naïf, preferring not to address the philosophical,
even while she closes with a, dare we say,
almost *mystical* observation.

My Teeth, My Breath:
An Unusual Relationship

I don't brush my teeth. No, really!
My teeth are so white
and I don't like them to feel too slippery,
but I do use Listerine and I do floss every day.
     But,

I don't brush them every day.
I'll use a shirt or something.
I know it's gross but I always have fresh breath.

It's really weird,
     but

I have great breath.

KATHY GRIFFIN
b. 1960

In this stunning homage to e. e. cummings, Kathy Griffin
plays with the reader, using intricate line breaks,
idiosyncratic punctuation, and an exuberant overall style.
Note the charming neurotic undertone.

ee cummings, renee and me (too)

get
this.
- i am a fan of renee zellweger because everybody
is   because i'm   human, everyone
is
(i loved her in
jerry maguire,) then i
seemed to notice
something happened to her face   where it seem to
swell up
to a point where she could barely verbalize
and i made a very ill timed joke (in people magazine)
that
she looked like
a
sweaty

puppy

    coke

        whore.

        Now that's obviously an exaggeration.

-however it does seem to be a

      fact   that her face looks

remarkably different than it did in

        jerry

maguire and yet she's very thin

    with a rather full face and her eyes are getting, sort of

    , smaller

    ? i'm not sure

    but obviously she's in some sort of a workout

      regimen - some may call it bulimia -

    -i

    would.

    -my mouth to god's ears,

    could i just get

    t

    hat

    bulimia

    at least for

    two

    weeks?

-but, anyway, i made that horrible joke about her
    and two weeks later
, she
    sent me those flowers—if you turn and see those
    roses?—with a note that seriously said,
warmest wishes,   renee zellwegger,   isn't that
    chilling?

    -so
    to this day   , -i don't know
    which
    way
    t
    hat
    could
    have gone.

THE "I'M NOT GAY" SCHOOL

*T*he "I'm Not Gay" School of poetry is a small but outspoken subset of the Explanatory School. These poets (usually male) home in on very specific subject matter, viz., the state of not being a homosexual.

Typical hallmarks of poems in this school are repetition of a phrase (most often, the simple "I'm not gay"), explanatory exposition, and a confiding, almost intimate, tone, as if the poet is looking into the reader's eyes and speaking directly to him, iterating and reiterating that very important point: I'm not gay. Really.

SIMON VAN KEMPEN
b. 1964

In his "Simon Says," reality-TV-husband/poet Simon van Kempen combines a confrontational style with sly intellectual humor. Note his clever paraphrasing of philosopher Rene Descartes's *"cogito, ergo sum"* followed by a tip of the hat to writer Jorge Luis Borges ("I am Simon" will remind the astute reader of Borges's "I am the river. . . . I unfortunately am Borges.").

Simon Says "I'm Not Gay"

If I was gay, I would be gay,
    but I'm not!
I don't want to have sex with men!
If other manifestations of gay means
    that I like to wear nice clothes and go shopping,
    then I guess that's fine!
I love fashion, but I love my beautiful wife.
    That makes me gay?
I mean, I've worn Speedos—therefore, I must be gay!
. . . I am Simon,
I am
    not
        anything
            more
                than
                    that.

J.C. CHASEZ
b. 1976

Singer J.C. Chasez takes a traditionalist approach, focusing not on the broader Aristotelian relational attributes of what constitutes gayness but on the personal "we're just good friends" trope.

This Guy Who Is My Friend But . . .

Let's clear that up real quickly
And the thing is,
We don't even get to hang out that much.
We are friends,
                absolutely,
The guy is a super nice guy and he's a friend of mine
                but
You know the only time people would usually see us
    together is in some type of photograph
                so
They just assume that it's like that.
You know people hang out with their best friends every
    day . . .

                and I don't even see this guy every day.

SHEMAR MOORE
b. 1970

Poet/actor Shemar Moore breaks a bit with the norm by using one specific incident—a photograph of him on a nude beach— as the focal point for his starkly simple and ultimately very convincing "I'm Not Gay" poem.

On Frolicking in the Nude on a Gay Beach

People find it interesting to try to make me gay;
　　I'm not gay.
I went on vacation with two girlfriends of mine
　　who, interestingly enough, got cut out of the pictures.
We found a nude beach, as far as I know,
　　was a unisex beach.

THE "I'M RICH!"
POETS

"The rich are different from you and me," said writer F. Scott Fitzgerald. And it is this that makes the "I'm Rich" Poets so fascinating.

These poets take a very simple idea ("I'm rich!"), amplify it ("I'm rich and you probably are not!"), and spin it into literary gold ("I'm rich and you probably are not, so I'm better!").

This is no easy task, but the "I'm Rich" Poets prove their (net) worth.

DR. MEHMET OZ
b. 1960

Dr. Mehmet Oz's poem, simply but aptly titled
"I'm Rich," deftly delineates the distinction between
the wealthy and others. A surgeon who also
plays one on TV, Oz wields his words like a scalpel,
cutting to the truth underlying his life:
He is not like "normal people."

I'm Rich (So I Can Spend Lots of Money Helping Little Animals)

[My cat] fell off some kind of a high ledge
and tore a bunch of these bones.
I saw the X-rays.

> Do you know how hard it is to fix
> the itty bitty
> bones in her paw?

I can guarantee
that normal people

> would not have been able to pay for it.

50 CENT
b. 1975

Rapper 50 Cent's quatrain evokes
a sense of mystery, even foreboding. The four lines
encourage the reader to wonder about the
"just in cases" that could occur . . . especially those
requiring twenty-five thousand dollars.

Small Change:
Fitty Times a Lot of Thousands

I always carry
        \$25,000 in cash,
just in case
        something happens.

MARIAH CAREY
b. 1970

Singer Mariah Carey takes a very different tack,
using her verse to dispute the concept of "difference."
In a fascinating twist, the very refutation defies itself—
resulting in a delightful poetic conundrum.

No Diva Am I

I had my team with me
but the pups had a mini-entourage of their own,
of course!
And why wouldn't they?
It was a big shoot and even my entourage had an
    entourage—
my stylist had an assistant, my security had extra security.
The shoot was based on the fact that some people think
    I'm a demanding diva.
I have no idea why people have that impression!

MARIAH CAREY

Here, again, Carey focuses on the "I am no different" concept—
this time in an exquisitely simple apologia.

I Am No Diva

Usually somebody else carries the bag,
because someone
once told me that
I shouldn't carry a bag.

JANET JACKSON
b. 1966

Who but a poet could take the banal—
a supermarket—and make it the stuff of dreams?
Singer Janet Jackson does just this.

Small Change(s)

I haven't set foot in a grocery store in years.
And that's so embarrassing.
I kept going "What's this?"
First of all I had the cart and I was riding down the aisles,
    standing on it.
And we got to the checkout and there's this square thing
        and I'm like, "What's this, you guys?"
        They said, "That's so you can use your credit card."
        And I said,
"You can use your credit card in grocery stores now?"

KATE HUDSON
b. 1979

Actress Kate Hudson's "I'm Rich" poem is a unique
one in that its emphasis is on the past rather than the present.
The style and topic are vaguely reminiscent of
Depression-era works, like "Brother, Can You Spare a Dime,"
as Hudson talks of the titular hard times and a
plucky child living through them.

*Hard Times for a Poor Girl Who Happens to be Goldie Hawn's Daughter**

It's funny, because everybody thinks I was spoiled and
  flew first class everywhere,
but it's not true.
My parents had four children and they weren't going
  to pay thousands of dollars for our air fares
—can you imagine the cost?

They wouldn't do that.
We didn't care—we had each other to play with
at the back of the plane,
while my parents were traveling in luxury
at the front.

*Who, thus, was forced to travel in business or even economy class.

MIGUEL HEAD
b. 1978

Many critics question the inclusion of Miguel Head
in the "I'm Rich" School, as Head is not truly
of the wealthy but instead close to them as press
secretary to Britain's Princes William and Harry.
So let us create a subset of the "I'm Rich"
School specifically for Head—
the "He's Rich" School.

A Royal Pain

The Prince of Wales
does not employ
    and has never employed
    an aide to squeeze his toothpaste for him.

    This is a myth
    without any basis
    in factual accuracy.

THE INFLATED EGO
SCHOOL

For the poet to produce truly good verse, he or she needs to find the right inspiration. Some poets find this in nature; others in history; still others in the philosophical or metaphysical. And certain poets find inspiration in one particular subject: themselves.

The Inflated Egoists (often admiringly referred to as the Nattering Nabobs of Narcissism) focus, laserlike, on that singular topic (themselves) which they clearly find ever-fascinating . . . even if others do not.

ALAN DERSHOWITZ
b. 1938

Lawyer Alan Dershowitz penned a nonfiction book
entitled *Chutzpah*. In the following poem—
an ego poem of implication—we can see evidence
(no pun intended) of said chutzpah in action.

Simply Me, A Humble High-Profile Highly Paid Harvard Lawyer

Most of the high profile cases are the most boring
      with some of the most boring clients I've ever had.
      They're just boring people.

The most exciting cases are the ones that present
      an intellectual challenge.
      For example, I had a case where someone shot
        somebody thinking the guy was dead.
      It turned out the guy he shot was possibly alive.
      Can you be charged with attempted murder for
        shooting someone you thought was a corpse?

I've been doing CSI before *CSI* was on television.

KANYE WEST
b. 1977

Rapper Kanye West's approach is a no-holds-barred,
no-prisoners-taken one. "Regrets" opens with a proud fanfare,
but it closes with a poignant and eminently moving couplet.

Regrets, I Have ~~a Few~~ One

I do have an ego and rightfully so.
I think people should have an ego.
Think about it—

> I don't offend people,
> I don't put anyone down.

> Do I name names or bring people down?

> That's not my thing.
> But I give myself big-ups.
> I feel good about the music I make.
> God chose me. He made a path for me.
> I am God's vessel.

>> But my greatest pain in life is that
>> I will never be able to see myself perform live.

AVRIL LAVIGNE
b. 1984

Uniquely qualified to write this poem, singer Avril Lavigne
sets the record straight about what inspires her.

My Unique Reflections on My Unique Self

I have my own style
that happens to be different from everyone else in
    Hollywood.
        My inspiration is me.

DONALD TRUMP
b. 1946

What can be said about businessman Donald Trump
that hasn't already been said? The poet himself manages
to find something new and, through bludgeoningly masterful
repetition, to turn this revelation into poetic gold.

Let Me Make One Thing Perfectly Clear

I am talking as a deal maker.
  I am a deal maker.
    I am a really good deal maker.
      I make great deals.
That is what I do.

DONALD TRUMP

In a stunning tour-de-force, Trump addresses
the same subject matter (himself) here—
even though he is theoretically talking about
fellow millionaire politician Mitt Romney.

NoncomMITTment

Well, I'm a much bigger businessman,
And I have a much, much bigger net worth.
I mean, my net worth is many, many, many times
   Mitt Romney.
And I don't know Mitt Romney.
I really don't know him.
So I'm not saying good or bad.

THE KIDDIE SCHOOL

A touch of whimsy, a dash of imagination, and a healthy dose of simpleminded thought—this is the recipe for a good children's poem. Below are some masters of this art.

These, the Kiddie Poets, as they are sometimes called, are not kiddies themselves, yet for some reason they have the unique ability to directly connect with their juvenile audience.

MICHAEL SCANLON
b. 1970

In rollicking list form, congressional aide
and convicted lobbyist Michael Scanlon teaches children
a valuable lesson on how to treat our enemies—
advice that will last a lifetime.

Kick Him, Beat Him, Roll Him Up!

This whole thing about not kicking someone when they
    are down is b.s.
Not only do you kick him
        —you kick him (until he passes out!)
        —then beat him (over the head with a baseball bat!)
        —then roll him up (in an old rug!)
        —and throw him off a cliff into
            the pounding surf below!

NICOLE KIDMAN
b. 1967

Actress Nicole Kidman takes a cue (and an opening line)
from the Robert Louis Stevenson classic "My Shadow"
as she teaches children all about body acceptance.
She boldly yet blithely accepts her own tragic physical
flaw in this, one of her best whimsical poems.

My Tummy

I just have a little tummy . . .
I think I've always had a little tummy, though.
It runs in the family.
My sister does,
my mum does,
my grandmother did. . . .
We affectionately refer to it as
The "little tummy."

DON KING
b. 1931

Boxing promoter Don King riffs on yet another
Robert Louis Stevenson poem, "The Swing," as he uses
his kinky curly hair as a metaphor for feeling special
about oneself. A classic read-aloud poem,
complete with fun sound effects.

My Hair Was Kinky Curly

My hair was kinky curly
like any other black man.
But when I came out of the penitentiary,
I had a rumbling in my head.

My hair began to pop up—

> *ping!*
> *ping!*
> *ping!*
> *ping!*
> *ping!*

Each hair reaching for the heavens,
straight and strong,
pristine and pure.

It was something I had nothing to do with
other than being chosen as God's child.
I don't know how it happened—
all I know is I go in the shower,
and as soon as I get out of the shower—

> *boom!*—

It pops right back up again!

MICHAEL SAVAGE
b. 1942

Talk show host and antigay activist
Michael Savage teaches tolerance and explains that
discriminating against others doesn't mean one
hates them. In fact, he explains to his
youthful audience that . . .

Gays Are Good!

I've had gay friends
All my life.
Currently I don't because
I don't have a lot of friends to begin with.
But one of my best friends all through my children's
early childhood was
A Gay Man.
An old friend of ours who would come to the house,
babysit.
We didn't care!
My point is:
Many, many gay people are
Wonderful People!

NEWT GINGRICH
b. 1943

Former Speaker of the House Newt Gingrich teaches
children how to count and tell calendrical time in this
quaint poem explaining how when he said various
things, he didn't mean what he said. This poem
also teaches tots how to prevaricate, a valuable
lesson for budding politicians.

Let's Count with Newt!

Well, let me say, first of all, nothing that I said in *The New
Yorker* disagrees with things I said
as early as
December of '03

when I talked about having gone off the cliff in Iraq,
things I said
all through '04
in trying to get the Bush campaign team to shift . . .
to concerns I raised in
December of '04,

January and February of '05 . . .
I don't see any other way to
read '06

except it was a defeat.

LADY GAGA
b. 1986

Lady Gaga takes a simple concept—the color red—
and teaches children that there's more to it
than meets the eye—*quite* a bit more!

So Many Ways to Think About Colors

If I decide to make a coat red in the show, it's not just red.
I think:

> Is it *communist* red?
> Is it *cherry cordial*?
> Is it *ruby* red?
> Or is it *apple* red?
> Or the *big balloon* red?

I mean, there's so many fucking different kinds of red!

CHUCK SCHUMER
b. 1950

Almost every child has had an imaginary friend.
Well, guess what! says Sen. Chuck Schumer . . .

I Have TWO Imaginary Friends

Biking through New York's boroughs in 2005,
I thought about some old friends, Joe and Eileen Bailey.
Though they are imaginary,
I frequently talk to them.

RALPH REED
b. 1961

How far can a boy go with his imagination?
Let's follow along with political strategist and former
Christian Coalition head Ralph Reed as he reveals his
inner G.I. Joe in this classic boy's poem.

The Dangerous Poem for Boys

I want to be invisible.
I do guerilla warfare.
I paint my face and travel at night.

You don't know it's over until you're in a body bag.
You don't know until election night.

THE LAMENTATIONAL POETS

---

*L*aments are among the oldest of poetic forms—stretching back to the Homeric Greeks and their sorrowful poems for fallen lovers and heroes. But modern poets, particularly celebrities, have taken this poetic form much further, lamenting the more poignant tragedies of modern life.

FLAVOR FLAV
b. 1959

In this spare yet haunting verse,
rapper Flavor Flav addresses a moment
of regretful epiphany.

A Rapper's Ruminations on Running a Restaurant (Chicken)

Let me be straight up with you,

I went up inside there on April 2 and I found potato
salad that expired on February 28.
And it's then when I realized I can't do business with
this man

And I really hope no one ate those potatoes.

HEATHER MILLS
b. 1968

Heather Mills, perhaps best known as the former wife
of Paul McCartney, lets slip the dogs of poesy and unleashes
her angst upon being hounded by a neighbor
in this heart-tugging lament.

Doggerel: On Being Blamed for the Death of the Next-Door Neighbor's Beloved Dog Which Really Wasn't My Fault

I've had 18 months of absolute abuse
and they tried to ruin my daughter's birthday party
which I spent ages organizing,
    saying I killed the dog next door. . . .

Complete rubbish.

I ended up being in contact with the lady.
She'd said, to get something out of *The Sun*
    that the dog had had a heart-attack.
I chased back to the vet Tim and he said, "What a load
  of rubbish!"
    The dog had been ill for a while
    and dies of abdominal catastrophe on Sunday night . . .
That woman that did the story on the dog, if she's so upset,
  why is she standing there posing for *The Sun*
    the day her dog died?
What I just want to do is clear up a few things.

JOE BIDEN
b. 1942

With the following, Vice President
Joe Biden moves us away from a lament
to an elegy . . . of mistaken identity.

Your Dad, God Bless Her

His mom lived in Long Island
    for ten years or so.
    God rest her soul.

And—although, she's—wait
    —your mom's still—your mom's still alive.
    Your dad passed.

God bless her soul.

JIM CRAMER
b. 1955

The poet–financial pundit Jim Cramer
here hearkens back to the incomparable lament
of Dido in Virgil's *Aeneid*. He replaces the
classic dactylic hexameter with his own innovative
Cramerian Sporadic Kvetchameter.

Rueful Ruminations After Being Made to Look Like an Asshole on a Top TV Show, or Once I Was Somebody, Now I'm a Buffoon

As soon as he started, I realized
       Stewart was on a mission to make me look like
       a clown.

       I didn't defend myself because I wasn't prepared.

       What was I supposed to do,
       Talk about how often I had been right?
       Praise myself?
       Get mad?

I was mad, but I didn't want to give the audience
   any blood.
       The national media said I got crushed,

       which I did,
       and made me into

       a buffoon.

JIM CRAMER

The versatile Mr. Cramer here moves
away from the structured form and experiments
with free verse in this follow-up lament.

More Rueful Ruminations, Etc., Etc., or Once I Was Cool, Now I'm Still a Buffoon

They wanted to make me the Face of the Era,
and they succeeded.
Rick Santelli's a conservative. Ideological.
O.K., I get that.
But me? I was very
anti-Bush.
I'm a
DEMOCRAT
I've got the canceled checks to prove it,
and suddenly I'm the ENEMY?
Me? Me?

"CASINO JACK" ABRAMOFF
b. 1958

Neo-Beat poet (and former lobbyist convicted for conspiracy)
Jack Abramoff turns an acid tongue on his former friend
Newt Gingrich (who was, in effect, Kerouac to his Ginsberg) in this
lament ripped from the heart. Written in the form of a blues riff, this is
best read aloud over the sound of a wailing saxophone.

A Convicted Felon Riffs on the Fickleness of Friendships While Flipping Through a File of Old Photographs

Here's Newt. Newt. Newt.
    Reagan.

More Newt.
    Newt with Grover this time,
    and with Lapin.

But Newt never met me.

    Ollie North.
    Newt.

Can't be Newt . . . he never met me.

    Oh, Newt!
    What's he doing there?
    Must be a Newt look-alike.
    I have more pictures of him than I have of my wife.

    Newt again! It's sick!

I thought he never met me!

JAMES FRANCO
b. 1978

A simple poem from a complicated man
(actor, director, writer, student), "Two Tercets" addresses the
very real regrets connected with seasonal dressing.

Two Tercets on Two Garments

I don't wear shorts a lot;
I have really pale legs.
I wish I could wear shorts.

I don't look too great in tank tops,
I just look weird.
I wish I could sport those a bit more.

ALAN SIMPSON
b. 1931

The rather commonplace topic of this lament—
changing times and mores—is superseded by the critical
question that arises: To wit, did former Sen. Alan Simpson
deliberately misname Snoop Dogg and Eminem as a satirical
device or are the misnomers the result of a sensibility
"not on the cutting edge"? Scholars have come down on
both sides of this issue, leaving us, the readers,
to make up our own minds.

Modern Times: A Lament

I think, you know,
Grandchildren now don't write a thank you for
  the Christmas presents.
They are walking on their pants with their cap
  on backward
Listening to the Enema Man and
Snoopy, Snoopy Poop Dog.
And they don't like 'em.

JENNIFER LOPEZ
b. 1969

There are prices to pay for great art, as singer/actress
Jennifer Lopez here explains. Notice the poetic effect of the
harrowing last line of this poem, which leaves the reader
stunned and virtually in tears.

The Price

You know, there are days when you just don't feel like it.
And actors aren't like, let's say the crew on a movie.
> They can't just blend into the background and go,
> "I'm not feeling well today."

So we're held to a different standard.

We work for it!
> And we have better clothes,
> and nice shoes, too.
> Those are the perks, okay?
For our loss of privacy.
And for your mom calling you up crying, "You didn't tell
me you were pregnant."

RAHM EMANUEL
b. 1959

Politician Rahm Emanuel's sonnet is Shakespeare by way of David Mamet—a formal sonnet phrased in *extremely* vigorous modern vernacular.

A Shakespeare Behind the Beltway Sonnet

Shut the fuck up and listen to me for one second, Rod.
And I want you to listen carefully, because this is the last
    time I'm ever going to talk to you.
You are fucking dead to me. You been fucking dead to
    Barack since '06, now you're dead to me.
Know what that means?

That means you're dead to my people in Chicago, Daley
    on down,
and all these friends you think you have aren't gonna touch
    you with a ten-foot fucking pole.
Listen up asshole. The shit's gonna hit the fan,
maybe tomorrow, maybe next month,

and when Fitz finally brings down the hammer
It's gonna be my name that's going through your head.
You won't know the hows or the fucking whys,
but it's gonna have my fucking fingerprints all over it.

Have a great life,
fatso.

RAMSAY

THE LYRICISTS

---

*W*ielding the precisely chosen word like a surgeon wields a scalpel, the Lyricists are noted for their rhetorical brilliance. Their poems are marked by an almost musical character. As such, many are best read aloud to fully savor the mellifluous sounds of the words.

PETE STARK
b. 1931

After being asked by a fellow congressman to "shut up," Rep. Pete Stark movingly and melodically expressed his feelings in the following. Particularly effective is his masterful use of the repeated word *fruitcake*.

In the August Chambers of Congress

You think you are big enough to make me,
you little wimp?
Come on, come over here and make me, I dare you . . .
You little fruitcake.
You little fruitcake.
I said you are a fruitcake.

GORDON RAMSAY
b. 1966

Chef Gordon Ramsay serves up this *amuse-bouche* of a poem—a short yet perfectly phrased mouthful.

Homage to Gone with the Wind

As long as I have
a hole in my butt
you will never deep-fry new potatoes again.

EMMITT SMITH
b. 1969

In the following "blow-viation," former football player turned commentator Emmitt Smith tackles an inspirational subject—the importance of perspective—in an unusually rhythmic way.

Blowing It

Don't worry
    about the game you just won
    or the team that we just
    blew out
    —or, um, blown—
    blowed out.

Let's think
    about what we need to do
    going forward,
    and they had, uh—
    blown out.

JESSE JACKSON
b. 1941

Rev. Jesse Jackson takes us to an open mic poetry slam in the following pithy and punchy verse.

Open Mic Night

See,
Barack's been talking down
to black people
on this faith-based . . .

I want to cut his nuts off.

JOE LIEBERMAN
b. 1942

This complex and majestic poem by Sen. Joe Lieberman takes parallelism and analogy much, much further than most, comparing our time (now) to many different "thens." Lieberman posits the questions: When is now? Is now 1942? Or 1930? Is now now?

Comparisons

There are people who have spoken
of this moment in history
as if it were the '30s,
    and there are some parallels, I fear, there.
People say the war in Iraq is comparable
to the Spanish Civil War,
and the war in Iraq,
    to the larger war against Islamist terrorism,
comparable to the Spanish Civil War,
to the Second World War,
the late '30s
and the failure to grasp the growing threat of fascism
  in Europe
    until it was almost too late.
The painful irony of this moment in our history
is that, while in some senses it is
comparable to the 1930s,
it's also already 1942.
Because Pearl Harbor
in this war,
    has already happened.

REX RYAN
b. 1962

Percy Bysshe Shelley's "An Exhortation" immediately springs to mind when reading this minor masterpiece by New York Jets coach Rex Ryan. Of course, we must substitute football players for Shelley's poets, and Shelley's lizards do not figure in the poem at all. But (metaphorical) jackasses most assuredly do. By the end of the poem, the reader certainly understands what Ryan wants to see tomorrow.

A Fuckin' Pep Talk

What the hell are we waiting on?
What are we waiting on?
>Do you want it or not?
>Do you understand there's a price to pay?
>Can we have fun?

You're damn right.
I DEMAND that we have fun.

Now there's a difference between having fun and
  being a jackass.
Our defense was a jackass when we went to Hofstra.
>Eating a bunch of fucking cheeseburgers
>before we go stretch and all that?
That's being a jackass . . .

How 'bout our offense?
When are we gonna put it together?
When are we gonna put it together?

> Can we not run the ball down their throats every
> snap?
> Can we not throw it any fucking time we want to
> throw it?

Let's make sure we play like the fucking New York Jets
and not some fucking slapdick team.
That's what I want to see tomorrow,
do we understand what the fuck I want to see tomorrow?

Let's go to eat a goddamn snack.

THE MEA CULPA SCHOOL

*T*he Mea Culpa School is considered by some critics to be a subset of the Explanatory School, but others note the major new innovation by some of the more prominent members of this school—the deft element of whimsy.

The thrust of their poems is an acceptance of guilt via a creative and humorously inappropriate argument. In so doing, the poets are more concerned with imagination than plausibility, and we, the readers, are the better for it.

JEFFREY DONOVAN
b. 1968

Actor Jeffrey Donovan takes a rather mundane situation—a DUI stop—
and alchemically alters it with the introduction of poesy and Benadryl.

On Being Pulled Over In Miami Beach (After Swerving to Avoid a Parked Cop Car)

Sorry,
>   I didn't see the red light or your stopped car . . .

>   The only mistake I made tonight
>   was drinking Benadryl with three glasses of wine,

>   I really think I'm only borderline
and not too drunk.

DAVID VITTER
b. 1961

Sen. David Vitter's poems bring to mind literary magazine *Kenyon Review*'s comment on the confessional poetry of Robert Lowell: "For these poems, the question of propriety no longer exists." Vitter impressively goes several steps further than Lowell, abandoning decency and dignity as well.

On Being Exposed for Wearing Diapers with a Prostitute: A Family Values Senator's Poetic Lament, with the Fortunate Understanding of God, to Whom the Senator Appears to Have a Direct Line

i. The poet first expresses his basic philosophy:

I'm a conservative
who opposes
radically redefining
        marriage—
the most important social institution
in human history . . .

I have no skeletons
        in my closet.

ii. After being accused of having the "skeleton" of wearing diapers and consorting with a prostitute, the poet attacks:

> The accusations are
> > Absolutely and
> > completely
> > untrue
> > just crass Louisiana politics.

iii. A short while later, the poet admits the truth, he indeed wore diapers with a prostitute, perhaps violating his strong family values stance, but God understands:

This was a very serious sin
> in my past
for which I am, of course, completely responsible
Several years ago, I asked for and
> received
forgiveness
from God
and my wife.

BILLY MCCORMACK
b. 1939

A fellow poet, Rev. Billy McCormack
of the Louisiana Christian Coalition,
weighs in.

On the Surprising Consequences of Senatorial Diaper-Sex

Vitter may well be much more able
    as a senator
    now than before
    because people tend to learn from their mistakes.

BLAGOJEVICH

THE MELTING
POT POETS

*T*he poetry of America is the poetry of inclusion; the poetry of celebrating that great American slogan "E Pluribus Unum." "Out of many, one." Yes, *everyone* living in our land should be included under the proud rubric "American"—be he or she Christian, Jew, or Muslim, rich or poor, white, or even, yes, even black. (And, in the case of possessing proper *official* documentation, even of Mexican origin.) This is the credo of the Melting Pot Poets.

BILL O'REILLY
b. 1949

Talk show host Bill O'Reilly, in one of his more sensitive pieces,
lyrically explores a revolutionary concept: Black people can sometimes
act almost like white Americans.

Dey Jes' Like Us!

I couldn't get over the fact that there was no
    difference between
Sylvia's restaurant and any other restaurant in
    New York City.
I mean, it was exactly the same,
even though it's run by blacks,
primarily black patronship. . . .
There wasn't one person in Sylvia's who was screaming,
       "M-F-er, I want more iced tea."

CHRIS MATTHEWS
b. 1945

News anchor and political commentator Chris Matthews similarly
explores this important blacks-are-just-like-whites theme and he does it
in an intensely personal way.

To Barack Obama with Love

You know, I was trying to think about who he was tonight,
    and
it's interesting:
He is post-racial by all appearances.
You know, I FORGOT HE WAS BLACK
     tonight
     for an hour.

WOLF BLITZER
b. 1948

News announcer Wolf Blitzer, on the other hand, demonstrates that he is not color-blind. Not at all. But he sure is compassionate about those folks.

untitled

You simply get chills every time you see
these poor individuals . . .
many of these people,
almost all of them
that we see
are so poor
and they
are
so black. . . .

ROD BLAGOJEVICH
b. 1956

In this charged empathetic work, former Illinois governor
Rod Blagojevich goes beyond color blindess to truly BE black.
(Ed note: Blagojevich is white.)

Black Like Me (with Apologies to John Howard Griffin)

I'm blacker than Barack Obama.
    I shined shoes.
    I grew up in a five-room apartment.
    My father had a little laundromat
    in a black community
    not far from where we lived.
I saw it all growing up.

RUSH LIMBAUGH
b. 1951

Is there a role for the new immigrant in the melting pot that is America? Here our poet-broadcaster, Rush Limbaugh, says ¡sí!— and proffers a time-honored solution.

Mexicanos Estupidos

If we are going to start rewarding no-skills and
STUPID PEOPLE

I'm serious,
> Let the unskilled jobs,
> let the kinds of jobs that take absolutely no
>> knowledge whatsoever to do,
> Let stupid and unskilled
>> MEXICANS
> do that work.

TRENT LOTT
b. 1941

Former Senate Majority Leader Trent Lott addresses the problem
of undocumented Mexican immigrants in a very different way—
by poetically proposing an electric fence. Much like ancient
Greek fabulist Aesop, he uses animal imagery to convey his point.
Can you guess who the goats are?

Electrified Fences Protect America: An Aesopian Goat Tale

People are
    at least
        as smart as goats.
        Now one of the ways
    I keep those goats in the fence is
I electrified them.

[*Moral:*] Once they got popped a couple of times,
   they quit trying to jump it.

JAMIE DIMON
b. 1956

From J.P.Morgan chief Jamie Dimon comes this bold and touching plea
for tolerance for another oppressed and hated group.

Can't We All Get Along?

Well, not all bankers are the same.
And I just think this constant refrain
   "bankers, bankers, bankers,"
—it's just a really unproductive and unfair way of treating
people.

      And I just think
      people
      should just stop doing that.

THE MODERN
METAPHYSICAL POETS

---

*M*etaphysical philosophers try to understand the very underpinnings of existence itself, the state of being and the world around us. The Modern Metaphysical Poets undertake the same task—but the questions they ask and the conclusions they draw are startlingly fresh and original.

Would an Aristotle, a Descartes, or a Kant have come up with these works? We think not.

LARRY KING
b. 1933

"What is there?" "What is it like?" These are the two basic questions asked by metaphysicians in looking at the world. Talk show host Larry King asks two different, but equally important, questions about the nature of existence.

Deep Questions

Why
     do people close their eyes
        when they sneeze?
       Do we still
    make razor blades
in America?

LARRY KING

King also addresses the time-space continuum (sans space) in the
following.

Poetic Conundrum

I've never thought too much about time
because
I've always been too busy
looking
at
my watch.

MILEY CYRUS
b. 1992

With wisdom far beyond her years, singer Miley Cyrus cogently delves
into the notion of an evolving consciousness while examining the
ontological theory of change.

Cautionary Words on the Transitory Appeal of a Diamond Skull

I'm very careful about the things I buy, because
      a year from now, I know
      I'm gonna look at a thing that I spent 30 grand
        on and say,
      "What the heck was I thinking?
      I don't want a diamond skull."

STING
b. 1951

Sting takes a more Eastern approach in his exegesis on the nature of authenticity. Or is it inauthenticity? He—and the reader—are left to ponder this.

Authentically Inauthentic . . . Perhaps

Nothing is authentic,
and yet everything is authentic.
So I think my work comes into that category.
But just the struggle to tell a story
in an authentic fashion
is already authentic . . .
and yet it's not.

JOHN MADDEN
b. 1936

In the following two metaphysical meditations, former sports announcer John Madden examines a monistic approach to being. There is no real dualism, he argues, in the first poem; but in the second, he admits a grudging acknowledgement of dual-aspect theory.

Meditation on Goodness

Well, when you're playing good football,
it's good football
and if you don't have good football,
then you're not really playing good football.

Meditation on Winning

I
always
used to tell
my players that
we are here to win!

And you know what, Al?
When you don't
win, you
lose.

JENNIFER LOVE HEWITT
b. 1979

Actress Jennifer Love Hewitt offers a bleak existential perspective on wearing heels.

Conclusions

I've run on my treadmill
        in heels
Thinking that it would make better leg muscles.
        It doesn't.
            It just hurts your back . . .

VICTORIA BECKHAM
b. 1974

Model Victoria "Posh" Beckham echoes Hewitt on the heels motif and draws her own uniquely Beckhamite conclusion.

We Are All on an Eternal Treadmill, Are We Not?

I have joined a gym but
I can't bring myself to start.
Obviously working out is important
—well, I don't—
What do you wear on the running machine?
I can't bring myself to wear flat shoes.

JERRY COLEMAN
b. 1924

Sportscaster Jerry Coleman tackles the core question of "beingness" by provocatively veering into cutting-edge developments of quantum-mechanical entanglement.

Lines on the Platonic Concept of Being

He just made another play
that I've never seen anyone else make before,
    and I've seen him make it
        more often
            than anyone else ever has.

DONALD TRUMP
b. 1946

Donald Trump's metaphysical work concerns itself with the act of understanding not only others' actions but the very stuff of human existence—the big wonger, if you will.

Reflections at a Public Urinal

How about the guys that stand there
    grabbing the urinal for balance?

I watch in amazement.

Then they come up and say,
    "I'm a big fan, can I shake your hand?"
And I'm a bad guy for saying,
    "Excuse me!"

They were just holding the big wonger,
and they want to shake your hand!

DONALD TRUMP

Ultimately, Trump moves away from the strictly theoretical to the real—
answering the always-asked question: "What is the meaning of life?"

Thoughts from Self-Purported Sagacious Self-Purported Billionaire

You know,
it really doesn't matter what they write
as long as you've got
a young and beautiful
piece of ass.

ALAN SIMPSON
b. 1931

Former Sen. Alan Simpson and interviewer Alex Lawson join forces in this masterpiece of Euripidean poetic dialogue. As did the ancient Greek master playwright, the two poets combine sophisticated counterpoints, parallel constructions, and rhetorical devices (shades of Lysias and Isocrates as well?) to create a dazzling sparkling gem of poetic political discourse. One only wishes to see this performed again.

A Poetic Dialogue Concerning the Social Insurance Program Funded by Payroll Taxes (i.e., Social Security) in Three Parts

Part I: *Adequacy*

Senator:
> We're really working on
> Solvency.
> The key is
> Solvency.

Interviewer:

> What about
> Adequacy?
> Are you focusing on
> > Adequacy as well?

Part II: *Bullshit*

Senator:

Where do you come up with
All the crap you come up with?
We're trying to take care of the lesser people in society
and do that in a way without getting into all the flash
  words you love to dig up,
like cutting Social Security, which is
> Bullshit.

We're not cutting anything, we're trying to make it
> Solvent.

> > (It'll go broke in the year 2037.)

Interviewer:

> > What do you mean by
> Broke?

Part III: *Picking with the Chickens, in which the places are inverted*

Interviewer:
Do you mean the surplus
Will go out and then
It will only be able to pay 75% of its
        Benefits?

Senator:
Just listen, will you
Listen to me instead of
        Babbling?

In the year 2037, instead of getting 100% of your check,
you are going to get about 75% of your check.
That's if you touch nothing. If you like that, fine.
You'll be picking with the chickens yourself
        When you're 65.

THE MODERN ROMANTICS

The Modern Romantics focus on the emotional and the personal, indeed the very personal. (Some have said the too personal.) Their work is marked by a breathless lyricism in their paeans to romance and—a particular hallmark of this school—a bold, unashamed addressing of the physical act of love.

KE$HA
b. 1987

Much as 19th-century Romantic poet William Wordsworth
wrote of "Perfect Woman," so Modern Romantic rocker Ke$ha
elegantly limns the qualities in her perfect man.

My Ideal Man

My ideal man would be funny and fat
with a beard.
I love fat men.
I like real men.
I don't like really feminine men who tan.
I don't understand that.
I like a funny man, though.
Russell Brand's not quite my type, but
if he had a fat, bearded friend,
that would be perfect.

> I could not bear to go out with a guy who takes
> longer than me to get ready.
> I don't want someone who's going to steal my
> moisturizer.
> I'm far from lonely. Far, far from it.

> But I don't want to settle down yet. Gross!

ICE-T
b. 1958

A speculative work by rapper Ice-T, "If" takes
the reader to a philosophical plane that is grounded
by an earthly sensuality. We indeed "feel him."

If (with Apologies to Rudyard Kipling)

If
a martian landed
and she was talking
the right
drama,
I'd be sleeping with
a green woman right now.
Ya feel me?

CAMERON DIAZ
b. 1972

Actress Cameron Diaz combines an unfettered
feministic sensibility with a philosophical examination
of the exigencies of modern love. Her last couplet
packs a particularly potent poetic punch.

I Go Where It Is

Oh gosh,

I can't even count how many times I've gotten
on a plane for love.

It's not unusual in this business;
my lifestyle demands it.

I'm always traveling for [REDACTED]*
You've got to go where it is.

*Four-letter "c" word referring to male reproductive organ.

50 CENT
b. 1975

Here, the rapper/poet 50 Cent
declares himself for the "higher love."

A 50 Cent/50 Dollar Sextain

I've been in hotel rooms, and girls were already there
    in the closet naked.
Hell, no! Are you kidding me?
That's like Amsterdam.
Amsterdam is fun for some people, but
I don't want no pussy that costs $50.
There's too many people that got $50!

JUSTIN BIEBER
b. 1994

"What I Like," written by pop star Justin Bieber, a member of
the Modern Romantic subset called the Innocents,
is especially notable for its use of vibrant and, indeed,
jarring juxtaposition used to a very strong effect.

What I Like

I really like . . . girls . . .
girls . . .
girls . . .
girls . . .
girls . . .
girls . . .
girls . . .
There are lots of things I really like besides girls.
Like pizza. . . .
And CHUCK NORRIS.

GIBSON

THE MULTICULTURAL
SCHOOL

A uniquely modern school of poetry, the Multicultural School concerns itself with the diversity that is the world today. Poets in this group proudly declaim about cultures, religions, sexual orientation, and races other than their own. These verses celebrating differences are often extremely thought-provoking and always highly sensitive.

LARS VON TRIER

b. 1956

In "Fey Comments," the film director–screenwriter
Lars von Trier gives a sly, friendly wink at anti-Semites.

Fey Comments Involving Jewishness, Hitler, and Film Directors Who Have Tongue Over-Cutely Placed in Cheek

The only thing I can tell you is that I thought I was a
    Jew for a long time
and was very happy being a Jew,
then later on came Susanne Bier, and suddenly I wasn't
    so happy about being a Jew.

That was a joke. Sorry.

But it turned out that I was not a Jew.
If I'd been a Jew, then I would be a second-wave Jew,
    a kind of a new-wave Jew,
but anyway, I really wanted to be a Jew and then I
    found out
that I was really a Nazi, because my family is German.
And that also gave me some pleasure.

So, I, what can I say?

I understand Hitler.

I think he did some wrong things but I can see him sitting
   in his bunker.

I'm saying that I think I understand the man.

He is not what we could call a good guy, but yeah,

I understand much about him and I sympathize with
   him . . . But come on!

I'm not for the Second World War.

And I'm not against Jews.

No, not even Susanne Bier.

I am very much for them. As much as Israelis are a pain
   in the ass.

How do I get out of this sentence? Okay, I am a Nazi.

As for the art, I'm for Speer. Albert Speer I liked.

He was also one of God's best children.

He has a talent that . . .

Okay, enough.

LARS VON TRIER

Von Trier takes his theme one step further in the following,
and cleverly switches from winking to groveling.

Not Enough After All: An Addendum after Negative Reactions to Fey Comments, etc. etc., Led to Being Banned from the Cannes Film Festival

I'm very proud of being persona non grata.

I've never been that before in my life, and that suits me
    extremely well . . .
I'm known for provocations, but I like provocations
    when they have a purpose.
And this had no purpose whatsoever.
Because I'm not Mel Gibson.

I'm definitely not Mel Gibson.

MEL GIBSON
b. 1956

Actor Mel Gibson favors a more direct approach.

I Am *Mel Gibson*

You motherfucker. I'm going to fuck you . . .
Fucking Jews. The Jews are responsible for all the wars in
the world.

Are you a Jew?
What the fuck do you think you're doing?
What do you think you're looking at,

Sugar Tits?

MICHAEL SAVAGE
b. 1942

Radio host Michael Savage turns his eyes to a different religious group—the Muslims. Interestingly, his harmonizing ideas seem to jibe quite nicely with those of the previous poets, albeit for this different group.

Kentucky Fried Poem

We are going to face this Hobson's choice.
People kept saying the extremists represent only
    10 percent of 900 million Muslims.
That's when I asked:
    Would you rather see 100 million of us fried or
    100 million of them fried?
    Nobody says this stuff,
so I say it.
    I'm screaming out from the wilderness.

MICHAEL BLOOMBERG
b. 1942

In this light, whimsical poem, the reader laughs
with the poet (New York City Mayor Michael Bloomberg)
at drunken Irish people.

Words to the Irish Historical Society

normally when i walk by this building
there are a bunch of people
that are totally inebriated
hanging out the window.
i know that's a stereotype about the Irish,
but nevertheless we Jews around the corner think this.

HANS ZEIGER
b. 1985

The little-known Hans Zeiger (who ran for Congress
in Washington State) takes a startlingly different approach
to the diversity topic. After reading this fresh voice,
the reader wonders whether he or she should
indeed find another cookie purveyor.

Musings on Girl Scout Cookies

The Girl Scouts allow
      homosexuals and atheists to join their ranks,
      and they have become a pro abortion feminist
         training corps.
If the Girl Scouts of America can't get back to teaching
   real character,
      perhaps it will be time
      to look for our cookies elsewhere.

THE NATURE POETS

*M*odern Nature poetry is not the gentle poetry of the great classic bucolic and pastoral poets such as Horace and Virgil, it is distinctly different in tone.

To use a nature-inspired analogy, the poets belonging to this school are drawn to nature like a fly is drawn to fecal matter.*

---

*Ed. note: Interestingly, the term, or variations thereof, has been applied by some critics to the end product of these poets.

NICOLAS CAGE
b. 1964

Actor Nicolas Cage takes us on a sophisticated
tour of the Animal Kingdom, utilizing
neo-Aristotelian categories.

Pigs, Not So Much

I love all animals.
I have a fascination with fish, birds, whales—sentient
    life—insects, reptiles.
I actually choose the way I eat according to the way
    animals have sex.
I think fish are very dignified with sex.
So are birds. But pigs, not so much.
So I don't eat pig meat or things like that.
I eat fish and fowl.

JOSEPH "BIG JOEY" MASSINO
b. 1943

Unlike Nicolas Cage, who eschews the porcine,
the lyrical mobster "Big Joey" Massino
savors it and eschews the piscine.

Vers Libre while Not Libre: Food for Thought, or Menu Choices in Federal Jail

I'm belching, I've got a lot of heartburn, a lot of agita.
I'll tell you one thing, that sausage wasn't bad, bo.
It wasn't bad, I swear to God.
I put a little mustard—
it wasn't bad.
I had no dinner last night.
I had peanut butter,
I couldn't eat.
Tonight,
I won't eat.
It's fish.

BILLY BOB THORNTON
b. 1955

At once a chilling look at the tooth-and-nail aspect
of nature (i.e., eat or be eaten) and an indictment of modern
television entertainment (à la *Network*), "On Komodo Dragons"
is an excursion into the darker side of the Nature School
courtesy of actor Billy Bob Thornton. This strong piece
may be difficult for some to digest.

On Komodo Dragons

Dragons are evil.
Komodo dragons have this horribly toxic bacteria in
    their mouths.
When they bite you, you go blind.

        Then they all gather around you
        and watch you die like
        they are watching television.

They don't eat you right away.
They wait till you die.

        Then they eat you.

DONATELLA VERSACE
b. 1955

Designer Donatella Versace, she of the never-seen-in-nature Boehneresque orange tan and enhanced lips, writes a wry, thought-provoking piece on the nature of nature. Is nature natural? she asks. And, if so, who cares?

The Nature of Naturalism

I don't even know what my natural color is.
Natural?

What is natural?

What is that?
I do not believe in totally natural for women.
For me, natural has something to do with

vegetables.

JENNIFER LOVE HEWITT
b. 1979

Here is actress Jennifer Love Hewitt's poetic homage
to the famed "madeleine episode" in Proust's
À la recherche du temps perdu, utilizing chicken instead
of the French pastry, but to much the same effect.

Eating a Chicken (But Not the Leg)

It's really weird—

I can eat chicken if
I take if off the bone,

but I can't eat a chicken leg
and have my teeth touch the bone.

It freaks me out.
It's just the chicken skin.

You go, "Oh gosh,
I'm eating a chicken,"

and it's really disturbing.

SLASH
b. 1965

Lastly, seemingly channeling the living spirit
of Virgil or Horace, rocker Slash invokes the bursting
fecundity of nature in the summer.

Summer Is Good

Summer
Everyone's happier in summer, . . . aren't they?
That's when the girls get their tits out,
that's when you get outdoor rock 'n' roll shows.
It's the ultimate party.
But you're unlikely to ever see me rocking Speedos
with my top hat!

THE PATRIOTIC POETS

The American Patriotic Poem—dedicated to the preservation of the American flag, freedoms, and way of life—has stirred American souls since 1776. Nearly two hundred and fifty years later, poets still turn to the United States of America as inspiration although interpretations of American ideals and, indeed, American history are sometimes refreshingly different.

SARAH PALIN
b. 1964

Although lacking the rhythmic beauty of Longfellow's verse,
this interpretation by Ms. Palin more than compensates
in other ways: a wonderfully stirring homage to
Paul Revere's historic ride, bells and all, that has
risen to the level of a classic.

The Midnight Ride of Paul Revere
(with apologies to Henry Wadsworth Longfellow)

He who warned, uh, the British
That they weren't gonna be takin' away our arms,
Uh, by ringing those bells, and, um, makin' sure
As he's riding his horse through town
To send those warning shots and bells
That we were going to be sure and we were going
    to be free,
And we were going to be armed.

LEELEE SOBIESKI

b. 1983

Actress Leelee Sobieski also takes on Longfellow—
offering up this reimagined "Hiawatha." Her strong images
break through the stereotypical and cause the reader
to feel he or she is with her on the shores of Gitche Gumee.

My Hiawatha

When I close my eyes and imagine what I look like,
I'm completely different.

> I imagine myself as a Native American
> in a canoe with a papoose around my neck
> and sitting alongside my warrior husband,
> my long black hair gliding through the water,
> my bow and arrow poised to shoot us some dinner.

[Then] I see my light hair and light eyes and it freaks
    me out, like,
"Where's my inner Native American?
Who took my canoe?"

NEWT GINGRICH
b. 1943

Patriotism often requires extraordinary sacrifices*,
as a former Speaker of the House explains
in this short modernist poem.

How Love of Country Forced Me to Enter Upon an Extramarital Affair

There's no question at times of my life,
partially driven by how passionately I felt
about this country,
that I worked far too hard
and things happened in my life that
were not
appropriate.

---

*Ed note: Mr. Gingrich has apparently performed this sacrifice for our country on a number of occasions.

MITT ROMNEY
b. 1947

Duty, Honor, Country. Patriotic sacrifices are
required of the sons of patriots as well, particularly in
times of war, as politician Mitt Romney explains.

My Patriotic Sons and Their Duty from a Pro War Presidential Candidate

My sons are all adults
and they've made decisions about their careers
and they've chosen *not* to serve in the military and
    active duty
and I respect their decision in that regard.
One of the ways my sons are showing support for
    our nation
is helping me get elected
because they think I'd be a great president.

TOM COE
b. 1951

A good American knows when to snap to (or zip up,
as the case may be) and do what is best for the country.
This is the key point spiritual advisor Tom Coe
makes in his brief yet inspirational poem.

To Sen. John Ensign: Good Old-Fashioned American Advice Given After a Family Values Senator Is Accused of Having an Affair with a Staff Aide (and Paying Off Her Husband)

I know
  exactly where you are.
I know
  exactly what you are doing.
Put your pants on and
  go home.

ALLEN WEST
b. 1961

This important poem by Rep. Allen West rallies us, like the
minutemen of old, to "lock and load" against birth control
and other terrible scourges that are causing the deficit to grow.
When reading this poem, don't be surprised if you
find yourself humming "Yankee Doodle Dandy."

Preserving Our Testicles

We need you to come in and lock shields,
>and strengthen up the men who are going to the
>>fight for you.
To let these other women know on the other side,
>these Planned Parenthood women,
>>the Code Pink women,
>>>and all of these women
that have been
>*neutering American men*
and bringing us to the point of this incredible weakness
>to let them know that we are not going to have our
>>men become subservient.
That's what we need you to do.
Because if you don't, then the
>debt will continue to grow . . .
>deficits will continue to grow.

JOHN MAYER
b. 1977

Musician John Mayer channels Lord Byron
in his lyrical recounting of love past, resulting in
(to paraphrase the poet himself) poetic napalm.

Pentastich on Jessica Simpson

That girl, for me, is a drug
And drugs aren't good for you if you do lots of them.
Yeah, that girl is like crack cocaine to me.
Sexually it was crazy. That's all I'll say.
It was like napalm, sexual napalm.

There are people in the world who have the power
    to change our values.
Have you ever been with a girl who made you want
    to quit the rest of your life?
Did you ever say, "I want to quit my life and just
    fucking snort you?
If you charged me $10,000 to fuck you,
I would start selling all my shit just to keep fucking you."

THE PSYCHOLOGICAL
(P)SCHOOL

*P*oets of the Psychological School—
playfully called the Psychological
(P)school by the major critics—are the psychic
diggers of the poetic arts, intrepid souls who delve
deep inside their own human psyches to uncover
the gold (or, depending upon the poem and/or
psyche, perhaps less precious minerals) deep within.

COURTNEY LOVE
b. 1964

Rocker Courtney Love describes the
costs—and surprising benefits—of drug use
in this sparsely evocative poem. High school
(pschool!) teachers, take note!

Calculated Psychosis

While the drugs screwed me up in a lot of ways,
They improved me in certain others.
I've never been good with numbers,

But

When I was on crack I could do math really, really well.
I became a fucking whiz at calculus.

But

I also became kind of psychotic,
Unfortunately.

CHRISTINE O'DONNELL
b. 1969

In this chilling little poem, Delaware GOP Senate nominee and Tea Party activist Christine O'Donnell takes us on a stroll into a literary Twilight Zone. Listen for the footsteps behind you as she manages to make suburban Delaware a paranoiac nightmare.

Follow the Leader

They're following me.

They follow me home at night.
I make sure that I come back to the townhouse and then
we have our team come out
and check all the bushes,
and check all the cars.
to make sure that—

They follow me.

CHARLIE SHEEN
b. 1965

Speaking of paranoiac nightmares, actor Charlie Sheen
has no return ticket from *his* trip to the Twilight Zone in these
lushly vivid sonnets that the great bard William Shakespeare
himself might have penned—had he been Charlie Sheen.

The Sanity Sonnet

People can't figure me out, they can't process me,
    I don't expect them to.
You can't process me with the normal brain.
I'm an F-18, bro, and I will destroy you in the air
and deploy my ordnance to the ground.

Um, Winning, anyone?
It's been a tsunami of media and I've been riding it
    on a mercury surfboard.
I'm tired of pretending I'm not special.
I'm tired of pretending I'm not a total bitchin' rock star
    from Mars.

The only thing I'm addicted to right now is winning.
They ask, will I do another movie?
Well, come tomorrow morning they are gonna rename
    Warner Bros. Charlie Bros.
They're all excited, I'm available, I haven't been for
    eight years.

I am on a drug—
It's called Charlie Sheen.

SNOOKI

THE REALITY SCHOOL

*T*he poets of the Reality School represent a fresh perspective in modern poetry. Many of their names are unknown or barely known.* Theirs are the voices of the often unheard, the "regular folks" who also are the so-called stars of what may be considered modern cinema verité.

Yes, we are speaking of reality TV shows.†

Given this, one may look at their work as

---

*Or only known for a little while.

†Ed. note: The term "reality" is used loosely when referring to these shows.

"poetry verité"—or reality poems: hyperrealistic, unvarnished, and always speaking in the voice of everyman.* We present a selection of their more important poems below—and we do so deliberately without commentary to let you, the reader, experience the immediacy, spontaneity, and naïveté of this refreshing outsider school of verse.

*And "everywoman."

NICOLE "SNOOKI" POLIZZI

STAR OF *JERSEY SHORE*

b. 1987

How We Demeanor

So all I'm saying is me dipsomaniac
As well as descending down.
That's how we am when we party,
Though the little of the things we do is,
      like, "Really, Nicole?"

We demeanor similar to the freakin' alcoholic.
I'm like, "You're sweating, your makeup is running,
We demeanor gross."
We usually demeanor similar to
      shit.

COUNTESS LUANN DE LESSEPS
b. 1965

Stigmata

I think that Quogue used to be, like,
    an *IN* part
of the Hamptons and it's just become
    not in.
It just has the kind of, like,
    low-rent stigma.

REAL HOUSEWIFE OF ATLANTA
NENE LEAKES
b. 1967

No Fabulosity Here

This is an event for the most fabulous ladies in Atlanta
like me and Sheree and Kim.

I don't know Phaedra that well,
but what I seen of Phaedra,
I ain't never seen fabulous . . .

When we talk about
fabulosity
I don't see it.

NENE LEAKES

Defending My Nose Job

I'm telling you that I did it
    and I like it.
I paid for it and I wrote the check and
  I'm wearing it, honey,
    and it ain't plastic, honey,
    it's all me.
I will NOT be getting a refund.

REAL HOUSEWIFE OF ATLANTA
KIM ZOLCIAK
b. 1978

The Rigors of Road Tours

Next time I go on a bus tour, I'm gonna
    get a bus driver that lets me stop every three hours
    to smoke.

I'm going to have like
    a chef on my bus for sure,

    and it's going to be clean,
    and new,
    and my ass is gonna fit in the potty.

KELLY BENSIMON
b. 1968

Real Logic

PETA isn't saying, "Don't wear fur."
PETA is saying, "Don't abuse animals."
And I'm not abusing animals.
I'm just wearing fur.

MIKE "THE SITUATION" SORRENTINO

STAR OF *JERSEY SHORE*

b. 1982

It's Lonely at Top (of the D List)

The scrutiny. And the microscope.
Obviously it's a blessing
—the women and the money and the fame,
   but at the same time it's
—it's actually very lonely. Very lonely . . .

When it comes to women, y'know,
obviously, they're throwing themselves at you
—but for what reasons, you know what I mean?

REAL HOUSEWIFE OF NEW JERSEY
MELISSA GORGA
b. 1980

Praise Song

I was taught to be
a wife in the kitchen,
a lady in public,
and a whore in the bedroom.
Praise Jesus!

THE RELIGIOUS POETS

*G*od stands with us all*, but perhaps more so with the Religious Poets, many of whom are billionaires or celebrities or former reality TV "stars." God has blessed them, and they in turn pass on their blessings with their profound and hauntingly beautiful religious verse.

*Except atheists.

LLOYD BLANKFEIN
b. 1954

Like Francis of Assisi before him, Lloyd Blankfein,
CEO of Goldman Sachs investment bank, is a devoted
Man of God, and this, his gentle poetic explanation of his
saintly role (and those of his brethren) in the outside
world, is his best known "little flower."

Trickling Down from God

We're very important. We help companies to grow
by helping them to raise capital. Companies that
grow create wealth. This, in turn, allows people
to have jobs that create more growth
and more wealth. It's a
virtuous cycle. We have
a social purpose. . .
. . . God's work.

DONALD TRUMP
b. 1946

Mogul Donald Trump shows us that there is much more
to him than the secular, plutocratic side we often see.
Particularly on holidays. And many Sundays.

I Always Go to Church Sometimes

I go as much as I can.
Always on Christmas.
Always on Easter.
Always when there's a major occasion.
And during the Sundays.
I'm a Sunday church person.

I'll go when I can.

DONALD TRUMP

In the following, we learn that Trump is not only
a church person. He also owns Bibles.

Bibles

I get sent Bibles by a lot of people.
Actually, we keep them at a certain place.
    A very nice place.

    But people send me Bibles.

    (There's no way I would ever throw anything, to do
        anything negative to a Bible, so what we do is we
        keep all of the Bibles.)
    (Actually I store them and keep them and sometimes
        give them away to other people but I do get sent a
        lot of Bibles and I like that.)

    I think that's great.

MARY J. BLIGE
b. 1971

Singer Mary J. Blige offers a modern,
urban take on the divine.

My God

My God is a God who wants me to have things.
He wants me to bling.
He wants me to be the hottest thing on the block.
I don't know what kind of God the rest of y'all are serving,
but the God I serve says, "Mary,
you need to be the hottest thing this year,
and I'm gonna make sure you're doing that."
My God's the bomb!

HEIDI MONTAG
b. 1986

Reality star Heidi Montag uses allegory
to draw the obvious parallels between her life
(complete with sex tape) and Jesus.

Me and Jesus

There were rumors about a sex tape,
  but I had nothing to do with that.
God knows the truth in all of this,
   and at the end of the day, that is the only thing
    that matters.
Jesus was persecuted,
   and I'm going to get persecuted,
   ya know?

MIKE HUCKABEE
b. 1955

Mike Huckabee, politician and talk show host,
explores his unique and close, yet oxymoronically
long distance, relationship with God.

While on the Phone with God

We know you don't take sides in the election. But
    if you did,
        we kind of think you'd hang in there with us,
        Lord,
    we really do.
  Yes, sir.
We'll pass those good words on.
  I see.
        You talked to the President, and
          he talks to you anyway.

MICHELE BACHMANN
b. 1956

Rep. Michele Bachmann similarly takes personal
calls from God—and shares the result in this poem
that focuses on God's heretofore unexplored
fascination with congressional politics.

When the Deity Calls

God then called me
to run for Congress . . .
In the midst of Him making this calling
sure,
what's occurred in this particular race
is that this congressional seat . . .
has become one of the top *three* races in the country and
you may have seen now God has
(in His own will)
(and in His own plan)
> has focused like a LASER BEAM after this
>> scandal that came up about a week or so ago
> He has focused like a laser beam with His reasoning
>> on this race.

JENNY MCCARTHY
b. 1972

Actress Jenny McCarthy shares a fresh
perspective on Jesus in her two-stanza poem and
definitively answers the time-honored question
"Is Jesus good date material?"

Two Deep Tweets or WWJD (Who Would Jesus Date?)

(1)
I'm looking at a picture of Jesus on the wall.
I would have totally dated Jesus.
Love that beard.
Too bad he's dead.

(2)
OK, OK, my friends.
I know Jesus is not dead.
I'm saying that the fact his body has "risen from the dead"
makes him un-datable.

EVA MENDES
b. 1974

Speaking of dating Jesus, actress Eve Mendes describes breaking up with Him.

Almost a Bride of Christ, but Not Quite (for a Really Good Reason)

I did—until my sister told me,
"You know, Eva, nuns don't get paid."
And I said, "Forget it!"

I've always wanted a better life, financially.

SILVIO BERLUSCONI
b. 1936

Former Italian Prime Minister Silvio Belusconi
has his own reasons, here poetically expressed,
for not following the religious path.

Arrivederci Jesus!

I'm no saint.

By now you've figured that out.

. . . There are a lot of nice-looking girls around.

THE SELF-EXAMINATION SCHOOL

*A*ncient Greek philosopher Socrates said that the unexamined life is not worth living. He was examining, of course, the great themes of one's life—morality, purpose, and meaning. But the modern Self-Examination poets (also known informally as the Speculum poets) go much further: Like stalwart space cadets, they boldly go where no poet has gone before.

VICTORIA BECKHAM
b. 1974

What does Victoria Beckham eat? Many have, of course,
pondered this. Here, finally, the answer.

The Truth Shall Set Me Free

I'm not going to lie—
I'm not one of those people
that says, "Oh, I eat hamburgers."
I eat salad.

NAOMI CAMPBELL
b. 1970

Sometimes the Self-Examination poet, in examining his or her own proclivities, asks the probing questions many of us are too frightened or existentially insecure to ask. This is the case in the following poem by top model Naomi Campbell.

Well, Huh?

I don't always wear underwear.
When I'm in the heat, especially,
I can't wear it.
Like, if I'm wearing a flowing dress,

Why do I have to wear underwear?

RACHEL BILSON
b. 1981

Actress Rachel Bilson answers
the "underwear question" differently.

My Memory Is Good

I've seen what the paparazzi can do
to someone if she's careless

about how she gets out of a car
and if she forgot her underwear.

Fortunately, I'm not one to forget about underwear.

Ever.

KENDRA WILKINSON
b. 1985

"Glamour" model Kendra Wilkinson is perhaps best
known for taking off her clothes. In this poem, she "takes off
her clothes" metaphorically—baring her innermost and
deepest feelings for the reader.

Girl Next Door

I was just a normal girl living a normal life in San Diego,
   California
       with my boyfriend who I was going to eventually
       marry,

Of course we had sex like every couple does
       and every now and then we would videotape it.
       There's a lot of couples who do that.

       At that time I wasn't a celebrity.
       I didn't even know
       I was going to become a celebrity.

CLARENCE THOMAS
b. 1948

Clarence Thomas digs deep in this little gem, explaining why
it is so fitting that he became a Supreme Court Justice.

My Life in Robes

I really don't want to be a judge.
I don't want to be judged.
I don't like judging other people.

VINNY FROM *JERSEY SHORE*
b. 1988

T. S. Eliot's "Love Song of J. Alfred Prufrock" inspired Vinny
to climb similar poetic heights. Rather than asking if he dares to eat the
figurative peach, Vinny, in effect, asks if he dares eat the *literal* peach in
his "should I or shouldn't I" poem about male-female relationships.

In the Vein of J. Alfred Prufrock

Do I dare write about it?
Do I venture into the cerebral territory where so many
    men have gone but failed? . . .

A big part of why men are not condemned as much as
    females for being conspicuous is that a vagina is higher
    maintenance than a penis . . .
She is carrying gold and he is carrying silver.

. . . Porn stars are a fine example of this system.
They are considered sluts but technically they are *selling*
    their gold every day.

> . . . So although she is getting pounded on camera,
> technically she is being rewarded for the goods that
> she possesses.

THE SPIRITUALISTS

*T*he more mystical counterpart to the Religious School (see page 204), the Spiritualist School takes a non-organized-religious look at the spiritual quest for paradise, perfection, and a symbiotic relationship with the Godhead. Thus, the personal God and personal concerns with God—as in the Jesus Date poems of the Religious School—are dropped in favor of the cosmic.

TOMMY LEE
b. 1962

Enlightenment and transcendent perfection are, of course, the ultimate goals of the mystic. Some, like rocker Tommy Lee, actually find it—and he generously shows us his path.

Paradise Regained

You must remove one article of clothing
—your pants, your top—
    or else you are not allowed in my dressing room.
So in order to come back and dance and party
    you gotta take off some clothing.
That gets the fucking party started so quick.
Everyone's walking around topless,
    and
        shit's going,
            music's bumping,
                girls are dancing on the table,
    and

        you're like,
            "Okay, this is perfect."

KATE BOSWORTH
b. 1983

Sometimes the poet advances his or her own prescriptions for achieving the mystical state, as does actress Kate Bosworth in the following.

Satori

It's amazing.
     Because if you, like,
          Have everybody taking ten minutes a day
And really focusing on, like,
     positivity
     and a better world
     and a better self, like,
Imagine all that,
     just
     all that
          positivity
          going out there?

KANYE WEST
b. 1977

This brief poem by rapper Kanye West
packs a powerful spiritual punch. One feels
he or she too is "home" at Gucci.

Past Life Regression

I won't go into a big spiel
    about reincarnation,
But the first time I was in the Gucci store
        in Chicago
Was the closest I've ever felt
    to
        home.

VICTORIA BECKHAM
b. 1974

What connotes spirituality? Who better than
singer/model/fashion designer Victoria Beckham
to tackle this complex yet simple question?

Quite Spiritual

I'm quite spiritual.
I'm very good at visualization.
I was talking to Gordon Ramsay and David about
    this and they're the same.
Gordon visualises a meal, then prepares it.
David visualizes the goal.
I'll lie in bed and think, "What kind of look do
    I want tomorrow?"

THE STRUCTURALISTS

*T*he Structuralists are noted for the structural complexity or innovative beauty of their poems. Among their practitioners, Pamela Anderson naturally springs to mind, but a number of others show similar technical virtuosity.

WAKA FLOCKA FLAME
b. 1986

With this intricate poem, rapper Waka Flocka Flame
proves that he is indeed "ahead of y'all"—
and ahead of the reader as well.

Like Bro, I'mma, Y'all:
Sharp Yet Random Ruminations

Like damn, my brain like so—
like bro, I'm so sharp.
Bro, I could play Scooby
on the camera—
then they think I'm dumb . . .
So really y'all just playin' y'all self.
Y'all in a ring with y'all self. . . .
So I'mma play mind games with them . . .
But bro, I'm so ahead of y'all . . .

PAMELA ANDERSON
b. 1967

Actress Pamela Anderson uses a variation
on parallel construction, opening with a declarative
"I guess" sentence, then closing with one as well.
Unlike Ms. Anderson, the reader surely "gets it."

Thoughts on a Dumb Blonde Stereotype

I guess ignorance is bliss—

When I do interviews people always say,
"Aren't you upset that people make fun of you?"
And I'm like,
"Are they making fun of me?"

I guess I just don't get it.

JAN BREWER
b. 1944

Note how Arizona governor Jan Brewer
uses a highly structured form to evolve from
the past participle to the past tense.

We Have Did

I have, uh, done so much

> and I just cannot believe that we have changed
> everything
> since I have become your governor in the last
> 600 days.
> Arizona has been brought back from its abyss.
> We have cut the budget.
> We have balanced the budget and
> we are moving forward.

We have done everything we could possibly do.

We have did what was right for Arizona.

TAYLOR MOMSEN
b. 1993

The following—a technical tour de force by
self-styled rocker/actress Taylor Momsen—is, one must say,
"totally" brilliant with its formalized use of adverbs.

Totally Taylor

I see myself as totally insane.
I'm totally moody.
Of course.
And I'm totally out of my mind.
And I'm always
      myself.

BECK

THE SURREALISTS

---

*T*he Surrealists challenge the reader's world view with an off-kilter, even warped, reality of their own. What is real and what is unreal? they ask. The reader will ask the same question.

LADY GAGA
b. 1986

Singer Lady Gaga has a mole. As with everything else about
her life, she tells us about it. But there's a twist . . .

The Dark Side of the Mole

My mole is on the other side of face.
My fake mole,
it's not fake
it's surreal.

    It's a surrealist mole.

LADY GAGA

Lady Gaga also has a vagina. And again, she is telling us about it.
And again, there is a surrealistic twist . . .

Excessively Surrealist Thoughts from a Surrealistic (If I Say So Myself) Artist (If I Say So Myself)

I have this weird thing
that if I sleep with someone
they're going to take my creativity
through my vagina.

JOAQUIN PHOENIX
b. 1974

Actor Joaquin Phoenix's "Frog Poem" is not
so much about frogs as about actor Joaquin Phoenix.
An added surrealistic layer: To whom is Joaquin
addressing his question? And, furthermore,
does it really matter?

Frog Poem

Do I have a large frog in my hair?
Something's crawling out of my scalp . . .
    I feel it.
I'm not worried about the looks.
I'm worried about the sensation of my brain being eaten . . .
    What did you ask me?

GLENN BECK
b. 1964

Pundit Glenn Beck is the undeniable master of the
eerie surrealistic poem. The Ken poems here are vintage
Beck—we read them with increasing unease and
rising horror. Who is this mysterious Ken, we first wonder.
Then "Who is the man behind the poem?"
In both cases, we say—it's Beck, all Beck.
Two as one, a multiplicity as one.

The Ken Poems

I.

Oh my gosh.

Ken,

I've gotta tell you something. I,

I,

I,

uh,

want someone.

> I'm not an investigator,

> I'm not an investigative reporter.

> I'm not somebody who is, you know,

>> on the bandwagon

> on cause after cause after cause.

>> Even though it feels like it lately,

I'm not that guy.

II.

I gotta tell you, Ken,

I,

uh,

you sound like a credible guy but

this, I feel like I'm in the same nightmare with ya.

      I can't believe this story is true.

      I ca . . .

      I,

      I

      don't . . .

if this is happening again inside of my country except the

   wishes are known and the person

      is not in a persistent vegetative state,

      is not in a coma,

if this person

      is being killed,

          quote, because

      she has

      glaucoma, and because

      she's old, and

      it's time to go to Jesus?

I've woken up in a parallel universe.

III.

All right. Ken,
we're going to
follow this story.
Um,
I want ya to,
I want you to
hold on just a second
     because I want to make sure we have
     all of your information.
     We tried to get a hold of, the
     uh, the
     granddaughter. But,
     do uh,
     do you
     have another way of getting a hold of her?
     She's, uh—

Her phone is not working.

THE UNRESTRAINED
SCHOOL

*S*ome poets are unafraid of how they sound to their readers. Unfettered by the bounds of usual self-restraint, they throw it all out there, so to speak, not thinking of how others might react or of what emotions their words may evoke.

These Unrestrained Poems are characterized by excessive or coy verbosity, insensitivity, or yes, pomposity that is transmogrified into great poetry.

For all these reasons, these controversial poets are often referred to as "The Twits."

RUSSELL BRAND
b. 1975

With lush prolix words and arcane allusions,
actor Russell Brand proves that a self-identified
intellectual can ably be a Twit.

Perhaps I Should Stop Sounding So Twee and Put a Sock in It

I'm very confident in the physical manifestation of a rocker.
And there are aphorisms I still deem tight:
    The carnal self is the true self.
In that barbaric, marauding period of promiscuity,
    there was
        a type of Aleister Crowley
        "Do what thou wilt" as the sum of the law.
That voice you use when you come? I was using
    it to perform.
Not some distant, attic-dwelling emotion brought
    out occasionally,
        like a front room you never use except when
            the vicar visits.
I was in there fucking all the time.

MADONNA
b. 1958

Madonna takes an unusual tack in her poem. She opens with a
confessional tone, then ends with an acknowledgment, even acceptance,
of those beneath her. The reader cannot help but be moved.

Housekeeping

I had to clean houses
—it was gross.
I had to clean the toilet bowls
of boys I went to school with.
No, there's nothing more degrading
than being someone's housekeeper. I mean,
God bless my housekeeper and . . .
well . . .
ALL my housekeepers!

EVA LONGORIA
b. 1975

In her short piece, actress Eva Longoria brilliantly manages to convey the agony of being a size I (smaller than 99.9% of the female population) while successfully alienating any woman of a certain size (i.e., 99.9% of the female population).

How Fat I Am

I'm not pregnant.
I'm just fat.
I gained 5 pounds over the summer
so instead of a size zero,

I'm a size
                    ONE.

LADY GAGA
b. 1986

Singer Lady Gaga takes us where we may or may
not want to go—back to her vagina, as is so often the case.

Should I Shut Up Yet?

I had all these number-one records,
and I had sold all these albums,
and it was sort of this turning point:
>Am I going to try and embrace Hollywood and
>>assimilate to that culture?
>I put my toe in that water,
>and it was a Kegel-exercise vaginal reaction where
>I clenched and had to retract immediately . . .

KE$HA
b. 1987

Singer Ke$ha—notable for cleverly using a dollar
sign in her name rather than an *s* to show how rebellious she is—
also shows how puckish her sense of humor is in the following.

The Christmas Spirit

Sometimes I'll walk my dogs
and fill bags full of massive dog shit.
Then I'll wrap them as Christmas presents
and give them to people.

NICOLAS CAGE
b. 1964

The Twit School sometimes overlaps with the
Self-Examination School, but with one very specific difference:
A poem examining oneself written by a poet in the
Twit School—such as the following by actor Nicolas Cage—
is not truly concerned with uncovering self-truths
as much as it is about presenting oneself in a
particular light (i.e., twittishly). Mr. Cage surely succeeds.

Cleverly About Me

I am not a demon.
I am a lizard,
a shark,
a heat-seeking panther.
I want to be Bob Denver on acid
playing the accordion.

GERARD BUTLER
b. 1969

Did you ever sit next to someone in a bar who wouldn't stop talking about his love life while downing drink after drink? Actor Gerard Butler vividly evokes this— and we are the better for it.

Women I Want Some of the Time

Sometimes along the way in my life
I don't want a smart woman right now, I want a dumb
woman.
But then you think, that doesn't work, now I want a smart
woman. Then
you get a smart woman and you go no,
that doesn't work
so it's just killing me right now.

COULTER

THE VISIONARIES

*T*he poet as seer . . . this is the mantle accepted and worn by the Visionary Poets. The Visionaries predict, prophesy, and foresee. Some of them are Cassandras, futilely warning of impending doom, others are Don Quixotes, dreaming of a different, more idealized, world.

PAT ROBERTSON
b. 1930

Polymath Pat Robertson is host of a national
TV show, the inventor of a special age-defying protein shake
(filled with energy-producing nutrients) that promises vibrant health,
and—as the following demonstrates—a prophetic poet.
In his "Warning," Robertson graphically warns us of current
scourges to be visited upon our planet by a loving redemptive God
in vengeful wrath for our love and tolerance of gay people.

On Disney World's Gay Parade: A Warning

I would warn Orlando that
     you're right in the way of some serious hurricanes,
     and I don't think I'd be waving those flags in God's
      face if I were you.
This is not a message
     of hate
This is a message
     of redemption.
But a condition like this will bring about the destruction
    of your nation.

     It'll bring about terrorist bombs;
     it'll bring earthquakes,
     tornadoes

     and possibly

     a *meteor.*

ANN COULTER
b. 1961

The Emily Dickinson of the conservative set,
pundit Ann Coulter does not follow the typical Dickinsonian
ABCB rhyme schemes in this short poem, but maintains
the melancholic acceptance of sad inevitability
found in Dickinson's later works.

I Have a Dream

If we took away women's right to vote,—
we'd never have to worry
about another Democrat president.

It's kind of a Pipe Dream,—
it's a personal fantasy of mine,

but—
I don't think it's Going to Happen.

GRAY DAVIS
b. 1942

Former California Governor Gray Davis's poetic dream
for California is ultimately so . . . Californian.

California Dreamin'

My vision is to make the most diverse state on earth
      and we have people from every planet on the earth
      in this state
We have the sons and daughters of every,
      of people from every planet,
      of every country on earth.

KEIRA KNIGHTLEY
b. 1985

Here the poet, actress Keira Knightley, imagines
the unimaginable—nuclear apocalypse. Moreover,
she boldly proposes a personal solution, one from which
we can all learn or at least carefully ponder.

If an Apocalypse Ever Comes

I'd like to be a skilled laborer and
not be left behind at a campfire
    making gruel.
    My friend's looking for a job
    and we found out you can get £15 to £30 an hour
for bricklaying.
I've found the courses
and the moment I have some spare time
    I want to do it.
        I'm sure I can find a positive experience
        in laying bricks.

JOHN BOEHNER
b. 1949

What if one is blessed—or cursed—with the ability to foretell one's own future? Speaker of the House John Boehner explains.

Frowny Face in the Future

A fella taking a thousand photos of
me.

> I didn't know who he was. And
> Finally
> I just gave him
> That Frown.

Of course, that's the one they're gonna use. And I told him.
I said,

> "This is the one you're gonna use."
> I told him.

Ed note: That was indeed the photo that was used.

THE WORD PLAY SCHOOL

*T*he Word Play School is concerned less with topic and more with mechanics. Metaphors, similes, outrageous imagery—they're all here. Prepare to be dazzled by their literary pyrotechnics.

CHARLIE SHEEN
b. 1965

Some critics place actor Charlie Sheen's "Gnarly Gnarlingtons"
in the Psychological (P)School due to its subject matter
(particularly the "Vatican assassin" delusion). But most agree
that its sense of fun and, of course, word invention
places it squarely in the Word Play School.
Let the reader be the judge.

Gnarly Gnarlingtons,
Assassin Warlocks, and Me

I'm not fair game.
I'm not a soft target.
It's over.

There's a new sheriff in town, and he has an army
of assassins. Oh, we must speak of the Vatican assassins.
Yes!

> We work for the Pope.
> We murder people.
> We're Vatican assassins.
> How complicated can it be?
> What they're not ready for is guys like you and I,
>   Nails,
> and all the other gnarly gnarlingtons in my life . . .
> that we are high priests . . .
> Vatican assassin warlocks.
> Boom.

Print that, people.
See where that goes.

JORDIN SPARKS
b. 1989

Singer Jordin Sparks invites the reader to explore
his or her imagination. "Who knows?" can be the only answer
to her conundrum of a question.

Who Knows?

I don't know why but
my bathing suit reminds me
of Fruity Pebbles.

REAL HOUSEHUSBAND OF NEW JERSEY
JOE GORGA
b. 1974

A brilliantly simple metaphor is at
the heart of *Real Housewives of New Jersey* husband
Joe Gorga's Word Play poem—which climaxes
in a strangely flaccid final line.

The Male Orgasm:
A Poetic and Scientific Analysis

You know,
you have this big white zit
and you finally pop it,
and it shoots across the room?
That's all this testosterone
building up.

DAVID WU
b. 1955

For a unique congressional twist on metaphor usage,
one can find no better practitioner than Rep. David Wu. Note his
elegant and seamless movement from "there aren't Vulcans"
to "there are Klingons to "there are *faux* Klingons."

When Metaphors Attack

This president has listened to some people,
the so-called Vulcans in the White House, the ideologues.
But you know, unlike the Vulcans of *Star Trek*
who made the decisions based on logic and fact,
these guys make it on ideology.

These aren't Vulcans.
There are KLINGONS in the White House.

But unlike the real Klingons of *Star Trek*,
these Klingons have never fought a battle of their own.
Don't let faux Klingons send real Americans to war.

JOHN MAYER
b. 1977

"My [REDACTED]" is, yes, about singer John Mayer's penis,
but it is also much more. His sly comparisons underscore
not only the state of male-female relationships in today's world
but also—in just five lines—touch on excessive
consumerism, civil rights, and, of course, the sense
of anomie pervading modern life.

My [REDACTED]:
An Appreciation

My [REDACTED]*
is sort of like a white supremacist.
I've got a Benetton heart
and a fuckin' David Duke [REDACTED]†.
I'm going to start dating separately from my
  [REDACTED]‡

Four-letter "d" word referring to male reproductive organ.

†*Four-letter "c" word referring to same.*

‡*See* *

RUSH LIMBAUGH
b. 1951

As Beat poet Allen Ginsberg vigorously and harshly
attacked the twin evils he saw besetting youth in America
(capitalism and conformity), so radio host Rush Limbaugh
takes on the evils of the 21st century (socialism and
classical studies) in this savage howl seemingly
ripped from his rotund body.

Rushbo's Howl: I Have Seen the Best Minds of My Generation

I have detected here what's really going on with all this
and how these sad-sack students are just a bunch of
dupes and in fact useful idiots. . . .

Now, do you think somebody going to college, borrowing
whatever it is in this case, $20,000 a year, to get a degree
in Classical Studies ought to be told by somebody at a
school that it's a worthless degree?

So here you have Miss Brain-dead freshly out of college
with her Classical Studies degree who thinks that she
wants to go classically study and that people also want to
study classics studiously and classically, and she's going
to be very hirable, very marketable and so forth.

Gets out in the real world and finds her only chance is
  Occupy Wall Street and to write a note for a TV camera
  about how worthless her degree is.
Well, that's what she does here. Her job prospects, zero.
  Yeah, they are, and they have been since you declared
  that major, and somebody shoulda told you that from the
  moment you declared the major in Classical Studies.

Tell me, any of you at random listening all across the
  fruited plain, what the hell is Classical Studies? What
  classics are studied?
Or, is it learning how to study in a classical way? Or is it
  learning how to study in a classy as opposed to unclassy
  way? And what about unClassical Studies?
Why does nobody care about the unclassics? What are the
  classics? And how are the classics studied?
Oh, cause you're gonna become an expert in Dickens?
  You're assuming it's literature. See, you're assuming we're
  talking classical literature here.
What if it's classical women's studies? What if it's classical
  feminism? Who the hell knows what it is?

 . . . Be very careful. If you go to college, do not do Classical
  Studies. What the hell is it anyway?

    . . . Karl Marx was a Classical Studies scholar.

ABOUT THE AUTHORS

*K*athryn and Ross Petras are a brother and sister writing team who fondly recall laughing at each other's early poetic efforts, most notably Ross's "Pinky Bee," which even by first-grade standards was lamentable, and Kathy's adolescent "Man-Smell," which is fortunately lost.

Inspired by the depths of their own literary output, they have gone on to collect the detritus and malapropisms of others—and published it in works such as the bestselling annual *365 Stupidest Things Ever Said* Page-A-Day® Calendar and *The Stupidest Things Ever Said Book of All-Time Stupidest Top 10 Lists*. Their website is, aptly, *www.stupidest.com*.